Bloom's BioCritiques

Dante Alighieri
Maya Angelou
Jane Austen
Jorge Luis Borges
The Brontë Sisters
Lord Byron
Geoffrey Chaucer
Anton Chekhov
Joseph Conrad
Stephen Crane
Charles Dickens
Emily Dickinson
William Faulkner
F. Scott Fitzgerald
Robert Frost
Ernest Hemingway
Langston Hughes
Zora Neale Hurston
Franz Kafka
Stephen King
Arthur Miller
John Milton
Toni Morrison
Edgar Allan Poe
J.D. Salinger
William Shakespeare
John Steinbeck
Henry David Thoreau
Mark Twain
Alice Walker
Eudora Welty
Walt Whitman
Tennessee Williams

Bloom's BioCritiques

JORGE LUIS BORGES

Edited and with an introduction by
Harold Bloom
Sterling Professor of the Humanities
Yale University

A Haights Cross Communications Company

Philadelphia

©2004 by Chelsea House Publishers, a subsidiary of
Haights Cross Communications.

A Haights Cross Communications ⚑ Company

Introduction © 2004 by Harold Bloom.

All rights reserved. No part of this publication may be
reproduced or transmitted in any form or by any means
without the written permission of the publisher.

Printed and bound in the United States of America.

10 9 8 7 6 5 4 3 2 1

Library of Congress Cataloging-in-Publication Data
Jorge Luis Borges / edited and with an introduction by Harold Bloom.
     p. cm. — (Bloom's biocritiques)
  ISBN 0-7910-7872-8
  1. Borges, Jorge Luis, 1899—-Criticism and interpretation. I. Bloom,
Harold. II. Series.
  PQ7797.B635Z7383 2003
  868'.6209—dc22
                              2003023937

Chelsea House Publishers
1974 Sproul Road, Suite 400
Broomall, PA 19008-0914

http://www.chelseahouse.com

Contributing editor: Elizabeth Beaudin

Cover design by Keith Trego

Cover: © Hulton Archive/Getty Images

Layout by EJB Publishing Services

Contents

User's Guide   vii

The Work in the Writer   ix
Harold Bloom

Introduction   1
Harold Bloom

Biography of Jorge Luis Borges   5
Amy Sickels

Writing against Time   51
Elizabeth Beaudin

A Modern Master   71
Paul de Man

Borges' modernism and the new critical idiom   79
Jaime Alazraki

Blindness: Alephs and Lovers   91
María Rosa Menocal

Chronology   133

Works by Jorge Luis Borges   137

Works about Jorge Luis Borges   141

Contributors   145

Index   147

User's Guide

These volumes are designed to introduce the reader to the life and work of the world's literary masters. Each volume begins with Harold Bloom's essay "The Work in the Writer" and a volume-specific introduction also written by Professor Bloom. Following these unique introductions is an engaging biography that discusses the major life events and important literary accomplishments of the author under consideration.

Furthermore, each volume includes an original critique that not only traces the themes, symbols, and ideas apparent in the author's works, but strives to put those works into a cultural and historical perspective. In addition to the original critique is a brief selection of significant critical essays previously published on the author and his or her works followed by a concise and informative chronology of the writer's life. Finally, each volume concludes with a bibliography of the writer's works, a list of additional readings, and an index of important themes and ideas.

HAROLD BLOOM

The Work in the Writer

Literary biography found its masterpiece in James Boswell's *Life of Samuel Johnson*. Boswell, when he treated Johnson's writings, implicitly commented upon Johnson as found in his work, even as in the great critic's life. Modern instances of literary biography, such as Richard Ellmann's lives of W.B. Yeats, James Joyce, and Oscar Wilde, essentially follow in Boswell's pattern.

That the writer somehow is in the work, we need not doubt, though with William Shakespeare, writer-of-writers, we almost always need to rely upon pure surmise. The exquisite rancidities of the Problem Plays or Dark Comedies seem to express an extraordinary estrangement of Shakespeare from himself. When we read or attend *Troilus and Cressida* and *Measure for Measure*, we may be startled by particular speeches of Ulysses in the first play, or of Vincentio in the second. These speeches, of Ulysses upon hierarchy or upon time, or of Duke Vincentio upon death, are too strong either for their contexts or for the characters of their speakers. The same phenomenon occurs with Parolles, the military impostor of *All's Well That Ends Well*. Utterly disgraced, he nevertheless affirms: "Simply the thing I am / Shall make me live."

In Shakespeare, more even than in his peers, Dante and Cervantes, meaning always starts itself again through excess or overflow. The strongest of Shakespeare's creatures—Falstaff, Hamlet, Iago, Lear, Cleopatra—have an exuberance that is fiercer than their plays can contain. If Ben Jonson was at all correct in his complaint that "Shakespeare wanted art," it could have been only in a sense that he may not have intended. Where do the personalities of Falstaff or Hamlet touch a limit? What was it in Shakespeare that made *Hamlet* and the two parts of *Henry IV* into "plays unlimited"? Neither Falstaff nor Hamlet will be stopped: their wit, their beautiful, laughing speech, their intensity of being—all these are virtually infinite.

In what ways do Falstaff and Hamlet manifest the writer in the work? Evidently, we can never know, or know enough to answer with any authority. But what would happen if we reversed the question, and asked: How did the work form the writer, Shakespeare?

Of Shakespeare's inwardness, his biography tells us nothing. And yet, to an astonishing extent, Shakespeare created our inwardness. At the least, we can speculate that Shakespeare so lived his life as to conceal the depths of his nature, particularly as he rather prematurely aged. We do not have Shakespeare on Shakespeare, as any good reader of the Sonnets comes to realize: they do not constitute a key that unlocks his heart. No sequence of sonnets could be less confessional or more powerfully detached from the poet's self.

The German poet and universal genius, Goethe, affords a superb contrast to Shakespeare. Of Goethe's life, we know more than everything; I wonder sometimes if we know as much about Napoleon or Freud or any other human being who ever has lived, as we know about Goethe. Everywhere, we can find Goethe in his work, so much so that Goethe seems to crowd the writing out, just as Byron and Oscar Wilde seem to usurp their own literary accomplishments. Goethe, cunning beyond measure, nevertheless invested a rival exuberance in his greatest works that could match his personal charisma. The sublime outrageousness of the Second Part of *Faust*, or of the greater lyric and meditative poems, forms a Counter-Sublime to Goethe's own daemonic intensity.

Goethe was fascinated by the daemonic in himself; we can doubt that Shakespeare had any such interests. Evidently, Shakespeare abandoned his acting career just before he composed *Measure for Measure* and *Othello*. I surmise that the egregious interventions by Vincentio and Iago displace the actor's energies into a new kind of mischief-making, a fresh opening to a subtler playwriting-within-the-play.

But what had opened Shakespeare to this new awareness? The answer is the work in the writer, *Hamlet* in Shakespeare. One can go further: it was not so much the play, *Hamlet*, as the character Hamlet, who changed Shakespeare's art forever.

Hamlet's personality is so large and varied that it rivals Goethe's own. Ironically Goethe's Faust, his Hamlet, has no personality at all, and is as colorless as Shakespeare himself seems to have chosen to be. Yet nothing could be more colorful than the Second Part of *Faust*, which is peopled by an astonishing array of monsters, grotesque devils and classical ghosts.

A contrast between Shakespeare and Goethe demonstrates that in each—but in very different ways—we can better find the work in the person, than we can discover that banal entity, the person in the work. Goethe to many of his contemporaries seemed to be a mortal god. Shakespeare, so far as we know, seemed an affable, rather ordinary fellow, who aged early and became somewhat withdrawn. Yet Faust, though Mephistopheles battles for his soul, is hardly worth the trouble unless you take him as an idea and not as a person. Hamlet is nearly every-idea-in-one, but he is precisely a personality and a person.

Would Hamlet be so astonishingly persuasive if his father's ghost did not haunt him? Falstaff is more alive than Prince Hal, who says that the devil haunts him in the shape of an old fat man. Three years before composing the final *Hamlet*, Shakespeare invented Falstaff, who then never ceased to haunt his creator. Falstaff and Hamlet may be said to best represent the work in the writer, because their influence upon Shakespeare was prodigious. W.H. Auden accurately observed that Falstaff possesses infinite energy: never tired, never bored, and absolutely both witty and happy until Hal's rejection destroys him. Hamlet too has infinite energy, but in him it is more curse than blessing.

Falstaff and Hamlet can be said to occupy the roles in Shakespeare's invented world that Sancho Panza and Don Quixote possess in Cervantes's. Shakespeare's plays from 1610 on (starting with *Twelfth Night*) are thus analogous to the Second Part of Cervantes's epic novel. Sancho and the Don overtly jostle Cervantes for authorship in the Second Part, even as Cervantes battles against the impostor who has pirated a continuation of his work. As a dramatist, Shakespeare manifests the work in the writer more indirectly. Falstaff's prose genius is revived in the scapegoating of Malvolio by Maria and Sir Toby Belch, while Falstaff's darker insights are developed by Feste's melancholic wit. Hamlet's intellectual resourcefulness, already deadly, becomes poisonous in Iago and in Edmund. Yet we have not crossed into the deeper abysses of the work in the writer in later Shakespeare.

No fictive character, before or since, is Falstaff's equal in self-trust. Sir John, whose delight in himself is contagious, has total confidence both in his self-awareness and in the resources of his language. Hamlet, whose self is as strong, and whose language is as copious, nevertheless distrusts both the self and language. Later Shakespeare is, as it were, much under the influence both of Falstaff and of Hamlet, but they tug him in opposite directions. Shakespeare's own copiousness of language is well-nigh incredible: a vocabulary in excess of twenty-one thousand words, almost eighteen hundred of which he coined himself. And of his word-hoard, nearly half are used only once each, as though the perfect setting for each had been found, and need not be repeated. Love for language and faith in language are Falstaffian attributes. Hamlet will darken both that love and that faith in Shakespeare, and perhaps the Sonnets can best be read as Falstaff and Hamlet counterpointing against one another.

Can we surmise how aware Shakespeare was of Falstaff and Hamlet, once they had played themselves into existence? *Henry IV, Part I* appeared in six quarto editions during Shakespeare's lifetime; *Hamlet* possibly had four. Falstaff and Hamlet were played again and again at the Globe, but Shakespeare knew also that they were being read, and he must have had contact with some of those readers. What would it have been like to discuss Falstaff or Hamlet with one of their early readers (presumably also part of their audience at the Globe), if you were the creator of such demiurges? The question would seem nonsensical to most Shakespeare scholars, but then these days they tend to be either ideologues or moldy figs. How can we recover the uncanniness of Falstaff and of Hamlet, when they now have become so familiar?

A writer's influence upon himself is an unexplored problem in criticism, but such an influence is never free from anxieties. The biocritical problem (which this series attempts to explore) can be divided into two areas, difficult to disengage fully. Accomplished works affect the author's life, and also affect her subsequent writings. It is simpler for me to surmise the effect of *Mrs. Dalloway* and *To the Lighthouse* upon Woolf's late *Between the Acts*, than it is to relate Clarissa Dalloway's suicide and Lily Briscoe's capable endurance in art to the tragic death and complex life of Virginia Woolf.

There are writers whose lives were so vivid that they seem sometimes to obscure the literary achievement: Byron, Wilde, Malraux, Hemingway. But most major Western writers do not live that exuberantly, and the greatest of all, Shakespeare, sometimes appears to have adopted the personal mask of colorlessness. And yet there are heroes of literature who struggled titanically with their own eras—Tolstoy, Milton, Victor Hugo—who nevertheless matter more for their works than their lives.

There are great figures—Emily Dickinson, Wallace Stevens, Willa Cather—who seem to have had so little of the full intensity of life when compared to the vitality of their work, that we might almost speak of the work in the work, rather than even of the work in a person. Emily Brontë might well be the extreme instance of such a visionary, surpassing William Blake in that one regard.

I conclude this general introduction to a series of literary bio-critiques by stating a tentative formula or principle for gauging the many ways in which the work influences the person and her subsequent, later work. Our influence upon ourselves is always related to the Shakespearean invention of self-overhearing, which I have written about in several other contexts. Life, as well as poetry and prose, is overheard rather than simply heard. The writer listens to herself as though she were somebody else, and the will to change begins to operate. The forces that live in us include the prior work we have done, and the dreams and waking visions that evade our dismissals.

HAROLD BLOOM

Introduction

For the gnostic in Borges, as for the heresiarch in his mythic Uqbar, "mirrors and fatherhood are abominable because they multiply and disseminate that universe," the visible but illusory labyrinth of men. Gnostics rightly feel at ease with Jung, and very unhappy with Freud, as Borges does, and no one need be surprised when the ordinarily gentlemanly and subtle Argentine dismisses Freud "either as a charlatan or as a madman," for whom "it all boils down to a few rather unpleasant facts." Masters of the tale and parable ought to avoid the tape-recorder, but as Borges succumbed, an admirer may be grateful for the gleaning of a few connections between images.

The gnostic gazes into the mirror of the fallen world and sees, not himself, but his dark double, the shadowy haunter of his phantasmagoria. Since the ambivalent God of the gnostics balances good and evil in himself, the writer dominated by a gnostic vision is morally ambivalent also. Borges is imaginatively a gnostic, but intellectually a skeptical and naturalistic humanist. This division, which has impeded his art, making of him a far lesser figure than gnostic writers like Yeats and Kafka, nevertheless has made him also an admirably firm moralist, as these taped conversations show.

Borges has written largely in the spirit of Emerson's remark that the hint of the dialectic is more valuable than the dialectic itself. My own favorite among his tales, the cabbalistic "Death and the Compass," traces the destruction of the Dupin-like Erik Lönnrot, whose "reckless discernment" draws him into the labyrinthine trap set by Red Scharlach the Dandy, a gangster worthy to consort with Babel's Benya Kirk. The greatness of Borges is in the aesthetic dignity both of Lönnrot, who at the point of death criticizes the labyrinth of his entrapment as having redundant lies, and of Scharlach, who just before firing promises the detective a better labyrinth, when he hunts him in some other incarnation.

The critics of the admirable Borges do him violence by hunting him as Lönnrot pursued Scharlach, with a compass, but he has obliged us to choose his own images for analysis. Freud tells us that: "In a psychoanalysis the physician always gives his patient (sometimes to a greater and sometimes to a lesser extent) the conscious anticipatory image by the help of which he is put in a position to recognise and grasp the unconscious material." We are to remember that Freud speaks of therapy, and of the work of altering ourselves, so that the analogue we may find between the images of physician and romancer must be an imperfect one. The skillful analyst moreover, on Freud's example, gives us a single image, and Borges gives his reader a myriad; but only mirror, labyrinth, and compass will be gazed at here.

Borges remarks of the first story he wrote, "Pierre Menard, Author of the Quixote," that it gives a sensation of tiredness and skepticism, of "coming at the end of a very long period." It is revelatory that this was his first tale, exposing his weariness of the living labyrinth of fiction even as he ventured into it. Borges is a great theorist of poetic influence; he has taught us to read Browning as a precursor of Kafka, and in the spirit of his teaching we may see Borges himself as another Childe Roland coming to the Dark Tower, while consciously not desiring to accomplish the Quest. Are we also condemned to see him finally more as a critic of romance than as a romancer? When we read Borges—whether his essays, poems, parables, or tales—do we not read glosses upon romance, and particularly on the skeptic's self-protection against the enchantments of romance?

The fantasy, "Tlön, Uqbar, Orbis Tertius," carries the Borgesian ironic esotericism to a sublime limit of ambivalence. Aesthetically, Borges is fascinated by imagined lands, since they are the ultimate instances of Platonism or Idealism. The Gnostic "Third World" or Imaginal Realm (as Henry Corbin termed it) appeals to what is most profound in Borges's own consciousness. And yet he was very wary of the ideologies that pragmatically manifested such tendencies: Marxism, Fascism, and all their variants. There is a perilous balance in Borgesian fantasy, which cautions us against the degeneration of vision into ideologies and political hellishness.

Borges's more strictly literary irony triumphs in "The Immortal," in which Swiftian satire, George Bernard Shaw's Creative Evolution in *Back to Methuselah*, and the dream visions of Thomas DeQuincy are fused into a parodistic nightmare that destroys both the Christian myth of immortality and the literary contest for canonical survival. Most powerfully, Borges turns against his own literary idealism, in which the identities of Homer, Shakespeare, and Borges merge into one another. A kind of horror, juxtaposed with fierce comedy, makes "The Immortal" a unique triumph of contraries, even for Borges.

The mysterious splendor of "The Aleph" again unites Kabbalah and Islamic esotericism with subtle Borgesian irony. The Aleph in one sense is a Kabbalistic and Sufi talisman, a microcosm that contains all multiplicity in a single, small icon. Daneri's poem (surely Borges was satirizing Pablo Neruda's *Canto general*) is a poor rival for the Aleph, and by ultimate implication, even Dante's *Commedia* must compare weakly to the Aleph, despite Dante's enormous imaginative achievement in a structured vision.

With "The South," Borges takes us to a border between dream and realistic representation. Dahlmann faces imminent death, or a dream of it. What matters aesthetically is the astonishing vividness and *rightness* of the story. Dahlmann is the emblem of Borges's own aesthetic dignity, of the writer's love of autonomy and of legitimate pride.

Borges thinks he has invented one new subject for a poem—in his poem "Limits"—the subject being the sense of doing something for the last time, seeing something for the last time. It is extraordinary that so deeply read a man-of-letters should think this, since most strong poets who live to be quite old have written on just this subject, though often with displacement or concealment. But it is profoundly self-revelatory that a theorist of poetic influence should come to think of this subject as his own invention, for Borges has been always the celebrator of things-in-their-farewell, always a poet of loss. Though he has comforted himself, and his readers, with the wisdom that we can lose only what we never had, he has suffered the discomfort also of knowing that we come to recognize only what we have encountered before, and that all recognition is self-recognition. All loss is of ourselves, and even the loss of falling-out of love is, as Borges would say, the pain of returning to others, not to the self. Is this the wisdom of romance, or of another mode entirely?

What Borges lacks, despite the illusive cunning of his labyrinths, is precisely the extravagance of the romancer; he does not trust his own vagrant impulses. He sees himself as a modestly apt self-marshaller, but he is another Oedipal self-destroyer. His addiction to the self-protective economy and overt knowingness of his art is his own variety of the Oedipal anxiety, and the pattern of his tales betrays throughout an implicit dread of family-romance. The gnostic mirror of nature reflects for him only Lönnrot's labyrinth "of a single line which is invisible and unceasing," the line of all those enchanted mean streets that fade into the horizon of the Buenos Aires of his phantasmagoria. The reckless discerner who is held by the symmetries of his own mythic compass has never been reckless enough to lose himself in a story, to our loss, if not to his. His extravagance, if it still comes, will be a fictive movement away from the theme of recognition, even against that theme, and towards a larger art. His favorite story, he says, is Hawthorne's "Wakefield," which he describes as being "about the man who stays away from home all those years."

AMY SICKELS

Biography of Jorge Luis Borges

An Unusual Perception

The internationally-acclaimed writer Jorge Luis Borges never wrote a single novel: his literary legacy was established on the many short narratives and fragments of essays that he composed in his lifetime. Born in Buenos Aires, Argentina in 1899, Borges always said he was grateful to have been born before the turn of the century, preferring to identify himself as a nineteenth century writer instead of a contemporary one. However, in truth, critics typically classify Borges as one of the early postmodernists. Prior to the publication of Borges's fiction in the 1940s and 1950s, most Latin American writers wrote traditional, realist novels. In the sixties, however, the literary styles began to change, quickly transforming the face of Latin American literature. Borges inspired not only important Latin American authors, such as Gabriel García Márquez and Julio Cortázar to experiment with style, subject, and language, but also made a lasting impact on the state of American fiction.

Borges's writing career spanned over sixty years, and included multiple volumes of poetry, essays, and stories. However, it was the fiction that he published in the 1940s and 1950s that most effectively challenged the pre-established, traditional structure and style, which led to his exalted reputation.

Borges's complex perception of the world derived from several different influences and events that directly impacted his personal life.

One of the most important influences on Borges was his early exposure to both English and Spanish literature. His love for books began as a young child and lasted until his death; books informed, inspired, and moved him. With his astute memory, Borges memorized verses and passages, and was able to quote from them at length. It was not only fiction, but also a vast variety of subjects, including etymology, mysticism, science, mathematics, and philosophy, that shaped his views and his unique approach to fiction.

Although Borges tended to live inside the world of literature, outside events also affected his writings. A witness to not only World War I and II, but also the violent government upheavals and dictatorships in his own country, Borges reacted against the disorder and chaos through his work. By blending fact and fiction, Borges reminded his readers of the power of imagination. He created imaginary and symbolic worlds that entertained questions of time, space, identity, and reality. Although he did not consider himself a political writer and in real life made several political blunders, his fiction effectively explored the realities and absurdities of society, government, and universes. Through his *ficciones*, Borges, always skeptical of dogmas, absolute values, or grand narratives, questioned and challenged the established doctrines.

Moreover, Borges's perception of the world was quite literally shaped by his failing eyesight. Borges's father and grandmother both went blind, and he knew it was only a matter of time before he completely lost his sight. At age 28, he underwent his first surgery for cataracts; by age 50, he was almost completely blind. Although the loss of sight contributed to his loneliness, Borges was not reclusive or asocial. He had many friends, and developed close relationships with those who cared for him. During most of his life, he relied on his mother for all of his needs, but in his later years, he valued the company of several different young women who managed his personal affairs and took dictation for him.

For a man who feared the idea of immortality more than the inevitability of death, blindness did not overcome Borges. It did not halt his love of reading or writing; rather, his blindness only changed the way he approached these functions. He relied on others to read aloud to him, and he composed his work orally, dictating his words to a secretary.

When he was fifty-six-years old, fully dependent upon others to read to him, Borges was appointed Director of the National Library. He was surrounded by thousands of books and could not see well enough to read any of them. Although Borges noticed the irony, he did not feel frustrated—he could still touch the books, open them and run his hands over their worn spines. He arranged his many books in his office in a particular order, so that he could retrieve them by their place on the shelves. He would pull a specific book from the shelf, and either turn to the page, quoting aloud from memory, or hand it to someone to read aloud.

Borges once remarked that his blindness gave him a chance to truly experience solitude:

> Formerly, if I took a train journey of half an hour or so it used to seem interminable, and I had to read or do something to pass the time. Whereas now that there are inevitable hours of solitude in my life, I've got used to being alone and thinking about something, or else I simply don't think and am merely content to exist. I let time flow past me, and it seems to pass differently. I'm not sure whether it goes faster, but it certainly contains a sort of serenity and much more concentration.
> (Burgin 44)

Borges, always fascinated by questions of time and space, now pondered the changes in his own perception of the physical world and his place within it. While his blindness muffled certain aspects of the outer world, his loss of sight also provided him a window into other realms of space and perception. As the exterior world turned to darkness, the loss of Borges's visual perception never threatened to undermine his mental perception. Rather, his failing eyes inspired him to pay closer attention to the places he could still see within his imagination. As Borges wrote about these possible worlds and multiple realities, he contributed to the transformation of the state of modern fiction.

An Early Bilingual Education

Jorge Francisco Isidoro Luis Borges Acevedo was born on August 24, 1899 in Buenos Aires, Argentina, to Leonor Acevedo and Jorge Guillermo Borges.

Borges's background includes both Argentine and Anglo-Saxon ancestry. The more distant lineage was probably Portuguese, and also perhaps partly Jewish. His mother, Leonor Acevedo, descended from a line of Argentine soldiers and freedom fighters. She grew up in a Catholic middle-class family in a house decorated with swords and military artifacts. Borges's father, Jorge Guillermo Borges, also claimed a military heritage—his father, Colonel Francisco Borges, was shot and killed in battle the same year that Jorge was born. Years later in interviews, Borges, quite proud of his ancestry, often talked at great length about his grandfathers' military battles. He liked to praise their courage and strength, while claiming that he lacked bravery; Borges could not entertain the idea that the act of writing could be compared to the act of fighting. The colorful family history, presented to the young Borges through tales and stories, webbed a fabric of ancestral mythology that illuminated his imagination early on.

Colonel Borges had married an English woman from Staffordshire named Frances Haslam, known to Borges as Grandmother Fanny. A wonderful storyteller, she often entertained her grandson with tales about the frontier days and about his heroic grandfather. Frances Haslam was a steady presence in his early life, and also provided a solid link to English culture.

The combined influences of Argentina and Europe began at Borges's birth and lasted throughout his lifetime. As both of his parents spoke English and Spanish, Borges grew up in a bilingual household. Jorge, his father, was a practicing lawyer and frustrated intellectual. He had made a few failed attempts at writing, and also taught psychology classes in English and studied modern languages. Jorge felt proud of his English heritage, and his library shelves consisted mainly of English writers. Borges's mother, not considered an intellectual like his father, was more closely tied to a traditional Argentine background. She was a practicing Catholic, while her husband claimed to be a Protestant agnostic. However, Leonor also felt drawn to European culture, and over the years, would cultivate her European tastes.

After they married in 1898, five years after their meeting, Jorge and Leonor lived with Leonor's parents for a short time. Soon after their son's birth, they moved to a house on *calle* Serrano in Palermo, an affordable and somewhat rough suburb on the northern outskirts of Buenos Aires that was notorious for its history of *compadritos* (hoodlums) and knife-fighters. By the time the Borgeses settled there, the neighborhood had settled down. However, the legacy of knife-fighters, tango-dancers, and prostitutes continued to color the streets and influenced Borges's imagination. Although he had no real-life experiences with any of these subjects, violence, outlaws, and knife-fights preoccupied Borges throughout his life, and they often appeared in his work.

Palermo was colonized in the mid to late nineteenth century by Italian immigrants. Working-class Italians still comprised much of the population, living in cramped one-story houses that typified the neighborhood. The Borgeses, however, resided in a spacious two-story house complete with their own water supply and a lush garden. The close-knit, upper-middle-class intellectual family rarely left the protection of their comfortable home.

Borges, called "Georgie," and his sister Norah, two years younger, were quite close. They did not have any other playmates and spent most of their time together, inventing imaginary friends, acting out scenes from books, and discovering new worlds in the garden and their father's impressive library. Borges wrote in his early book *Evaristo Carriego* that he finally realized he did not grow up in the slums but "in a garden, behind a speared railing, and in a library of unlimited English books." During the summers, the family vacationed at a summerhouse in Adrogué, a town south of Buenos Aires that provided a relaxed European setting for its residents. There, Borges learned to swim, the only athletic skill he would acquire. One of his favorite places to visit was the zoo, where he watched the pacing tigers. His early fascination with the Indian tiger turned into an image that haunted much of his poetry and fiction.

Borges did not attend school until he was nine years old. His father, an anarchist, libertarian, and admirer of the English philosopher Herbert Spencer's teachings, did not trust any type of state-run enterprise and did not want his children to be indoctrinated by the state's religion or nationalism. So, Borges's earliest education derived from his father, his grandmother Fanny, and his English nanny and tutor, Miss Tink.

A bookish and nearsighted child, Borges read both in English and Spanish. The first novel he read was *Huckleberry Finn*, soon followed by *A Thousand Nights and a Night*, both of which stimulated his imagination. Borges was exposed to English-language literature before he was to Spanish literature, and his literary diet consisted of many European and American writers, such as H.G. Wells, Edgar Allan Poe, Henry Wadsworth Longfellow, the Brothers Grimm, Robert Louis Stevenson, Charles Dickens, Lewis Carroll, Jack London, Rudyard Kipling, Percy Shelley, John Keats, and Algernon Charles Swinburne. Of Latino writers, he read the Argentine poet José Hernández's epic poem *Martín Fierro*, Cervantes (although in English translation), and books about *gauchos* (cowboys) and outlaws, which were much like American paperback westerns. His biographer James Woodall stresses how books helped to shape Borges: "Books were Borges's touchstone for reality, how he interpreted the world; reading was his first skill, his chief inheritance, and the foundation of a scattershot education" (Woodall 15).

Borges, precocious and quite well-read, also experimented with writing at a young age. According to his mother, he announced at age six that he wanted to be a writer, and during these very early years of his life, he wrote many imitative and plagiarized stories. At age nine, he published his first work: a Spanish translation of Oscar Wilde's "The Happy Prince" that appeared in the local newspaper, *El País*. The signature, "Jorge Borges," led many family friends to assume Borges's father was the author.

Also when he was nine years old, Borges attended public school for the first time, a traumatizing experience. As Woodall attests, the other boys took one look at this "soft-faced, bespectacled, stammering boy in ridiculous clothing—an Eton collar and tie—and knew they had a victim" (18). A mannerly boy who spoke English, dressed funny, did not like sports, and excelled in academics stood out as an easy target for the tough Palermo boys—they bullied him constantly.

At school Borges learned only Argentine nationalism; his real education, and his only experience with friendship, came from his family. When he was ten years old, his father began discussing philosophy with him. Jorge also taught his son the game of chess and presented him with mathematical theories and philosophical puzzles. Jorge's bohemian friends also influenced Borges's education. As he grew older, he had more contact with these men, such as Evaristo Carriego. A restless, self-educated minor poet and remarkable conversationalist, Carriego left a strong impression on Borges. Other rougher individuals also visited the home, bringing "something of the rackety, proletarian flavor of Palermo into the Borges household" (Woodall 19).

Even though the children led protected lives, they could not be sheltered from the events happening within their family. Their father's eyesight had been troubling him for years, and now he was rapidly going blind. Jorge had been forced to retire at age thirty-seven. He depended heavily on Leonor, who put up with his infidelities and held the family together. She was the rock of the family. Unlike her husband and children, Leonor was practical and realistic, and took care of her family for all of her life.

The Borgeses decided to travel to Geneva so that Jorge could undergo an operation for his eyes. Everyone in the family looked forward to the trip to Europe. Fifteen-year-old Borges certainly welcomed the change—it would prove a relief from the bullies at school, and, although he did not know it at the time, would serve as an important catalyst in his development as a writer and intellectual.

Ultraism and Europe

Although the Borgeses were not extremely wealthy, Jorge's savings and pension allowed them to travel overseas. They also lived inexpensively, staying in places with cheap rents. After a brief stop in England and then Paris, the family, along with Leonor's mother Leonor Suárez, arrived in Geneva in mid-April, 1914. The two Borges adolescents continued with their studies; that summer they were tutored in French. While Borges struggled with the language, his sister became quite proficient. Norah and Borges stayed with their grandmother while their parents started a European tour; however, war soon broke out. Jorge and Leonor only reached as far as Munich.

The original plan had been to stay in Europe for a year, but now that World War I had started, they couldn't leave. The family had been blissfully unaware of the pending war. Woodall states that while the Borgeses were somewhat out of touch with international politics, this attitude was not unusual: "The Borgeses were actually neither more nor less so [unaware of the political situation] than any other well-educated middle-class family of the time, though their being Argentine no doubt made them feel especially distant from the four-year conflagration that lay ahead" (Woodall 25).

In the fall, fifteen-year-old Borges attended Collège Calvin, a boys' day-school, while Norah enrolled in Geneva's School of Fine Arts.

The differences between Collège Calvin and Borges's school in Palermo were vast, and they were important in helping to shape Borges's personality. One noticeable change was that he no longer worried about being bullied. He easily made friends at his new school, and when he failed his first French exam, his classmates quickly defended him. They signed a petition for him to be promoted to the next grade, arguing that the headmaster should show leniency, since he passed all of the other subjects and French was still new to him. The petition was a success, both in terms of promoting Borges to the next grade and in bolstering his confidence.

The level of education also differed drastically. At Collège Calvin, Borges studied Latin, read extensively, and encountered Symbolist literature for the first time, pursuing the work of Arthur Rimbaud and Mallarmé. His long list of authors expanded to include Emíle Zola, Guy de Maupassant, and Gustave Flaubert. Although he read mostly European authors, he also continued to read gaucho stories and Argentine poetry. Reading consumed Borges, and in many ways, this was his most persuasive reality—not the atmosphere of world war. The Borges family guarded themselves from the war, happily continuing on with their routines. Similar to their abode in Palermo, their house in Europe served to protect them from exterior events.

Reading Thomas Carlyle's *Sartor Resartus* introduced Borges to German thought and poetry, and reading the German poet Heinrich Heine inspired him to learn German. Borges impressively taught himself the language, reading German literature with a German-English dictionary at his side. Soon the German philosophers Artur Schopenhaur and Friedrich Nietzsche also impacted his thought-process and philosophical musings. However, when he encountered, in a German translation, Walt Whitman's *Leaves of Grass*, the book moved him as nothing else before had. Whitman's effect on Borges's passionate feelings toward literature was immediate: "He elevated him beyond the status of a mere hero; Whitman became a household god, something to dream about and worship" (Woodall 31). While Whitman's writing taught Borges about intellectual rebellion and freedom, it was actually the German Expressionists who stirred the poet in him. At some point during his family's stay in Geneva, Borges began writing his own poems, experimenting with French and English sonnets.

Although Borges's intellectual and artistic life blossomed, his father worried about his sexual maturity. Before Borges turned eighteen, his father carried out a rash plan to send his son to a prostitute. The situation caused the adolescent Borges great anxiety, a feeling that was further complicated by the knowledge that his own father frequented the brothels. According to biographers and friends of Borges, the event traumatized and humiliated Borges, impacting him so severely that he did not explore sexual relations again for another thirty years.

The family had been living in Europe for three years and the Swiss eye specialist's treatments proved to be moderately successful for the elder Jorge. The Borgeses remained close and supportive of each other, and they were delighted when Grandmother Fanny sailed across the war-active waters to join them. However, not long after she arrived, the family experienced a loss—the death of Leonor's mother, Leonor Suárez, whom they buried in Geneva. The Borgeses discussed returning to Buenos Aires, but stories of street riots convinced the family to remain in Europe. In the spring of 1919, they moved to Spain.

They started in Barcelona, then moved to Mallorca, where they stayed ten months. Borges quickly made friends with other young poets, and continued to study Latin and read extensively. For relaxation, he went swimming. While his father worked on a novel, Borges also took up his pen, composing poems and essays. Although a Madrid magazine, *La Esfera*, rejected his first story, his first article, a book review composed in French, was published in *La Feuille*, a Geneva paper. By Christmas, the family moved to Seville, and although their time there was short, Borges began to live the life of an artist. He engaged with a crowd of local literati and became involved in the journal *Grecia*—the first journal to publish one of his poems, a long-winded one in the style of his hero Walt Whitman.

It was in Madrid, where the family moved in 1920, that Borges became involved in a literary circle that truly fueled his imagination and challenged his thinking about literature. The informal head of this circle was the Andalusian poet Rafael Cansinos-Assens, one of Borges's early mentors and inspirations. The intellectual Cansinos-Assens knew eleven different languages, and had a reputation for being an enticing speaker and passionate thinker. The young intellectual Borges immediately caught his attention: "Refined, equable, with the ardor of a poet restrained by a fortunate intellectual coolness, carrying a classical culture of Greek philosophers and oriental troubadours which attached him to the past, causing in him a love of notebooks and folios, unimpaired by modern marvels" (qtd. in Woodall 38). Cansinos's description of Borges reveals Borges's connection to literature of the past, as well as his intellectual personality.

Cansinos-Assens presided over a group of idealists and poets who gathered every Saturday night at the Café Colonial to engage in literary conversation. The group loved American jazz, and felt more connected to European, rather than Spanish, culture. At these lively gatherings, Cansinos-Assens would provide a topic, such as The Metaphor, and the group would bandy ideas back and forth. From this group, the movement called Ultraism was born.

Ultraism, like the movement of Futurism, concerned itself with manifestos, attitude, and ideas. The aesthetics focused on purity of metaphor and rhythm, and its creed celebrated the future and the new. The group exalted pacifism, anarchy, and free-thinking. Ultraism reacted against the self-conscious style of modernism, by reducing lyricism to metaphors, combining several images into one, and eliminating sermonizing; its enthusiasts treated the movement like a game. Under the influence of Ultraism, Borges wrote many essays and poems. Norah also became involved in the movement, publishing woodcuts in the Ultraist journals. The Borges children were not the only ones in the family actively publishing; Jorge's novel was finally completed and published in an edition of 500 (the cost of which was paid for by Jorge).

Although Europe positively affected the entire family, and in many ways the Borgeses embraced European ideals over Latin-American ideals, they still felt like visitors after seven years. It was time to return home; the Borgeses left for Argentina in March of 1921. Borges was twenty-one-years old. Although he knew he wanted to be a poet, he was uncertain about how his poetic aspirations would develop in Argentina—the place where he was born and yet hardly knew. Before leaving, he destroyed all of his Ultraist poems and essays, embarrassed by his youthful efforts. Even with his uncertainty about the future, he also sensed that he now had a chance to redefine his poetics and to grow as a writer.

The Literary Scene of Buenos Aires

Upon returning to Argentina, the Borgeses didn't return to Palermo, but moved closer to the center of Buenos Aires, in an area shadowed by a penitentiary, beer factories, and bars. In the family's seven-year absence, Buenos Aires had undergone many changes, and now thrived as a wealthy city with a population of almost two million. Under the wave of progress and modernity, new industries, such as mining and petroleum exploitation, were being developed, and subway lines provided urban transportation. The country experienced a postwar prosperity—revenues from the granaries and beef seemed endless. Argentina had also witnessed huge waves of immigrants, one cause of its rapid growth. With the population increase, more people began to demand government representation. Until the late 1800s the ruling classes, landowners and the military, had maintained a feudal system; in 1911, suffrage was granted to all men. In 1916, the Radical party swept the elections, and during this period the benefits of public education were extended to everyone.

Although Buenos Aires overflowed with employment opportunities, Borges did not look for a job. He had made the choice to be a writer, and his parents fully encouraged his decision to pursue the arts and eschew the workforce. Unlike parents of many young artists, Leonor and Jorge not only emotionally supported their son, but even financed him. Borges, in his twenties and living at home, expressed no desire to strike out on his own. He depended on his parents as he had for all his life. His mother even continued to pick out his clothes for him.

Although he did not move away from home, Borges did venture into new territory. He cultivated many friendships and literary acquaintances during the 1920s and 1930s. Shortly after his return to Argentina, he fell under the influence of one of his father's bohemian friends, Macedonio Fernández, an eccentric, intellectual wanderer. Fernández, an outstanding conversationalist, complex philosopher, and anarchist, traveled from boarding house to boarding house, leaving his writings behind from one place to the next. His philosophical ideas challenged and inspired Borges, and from Macedonio, Borges learned to read everything with skepticism, a lesson that stayed with him for all of his life. Similar to Cansinos-Assens, Macedonio also presided over a Saturday night literary circle—however, it was Borges who truly brought Ultraism to Argentina.

Over the next decade, Borges became deeply involved in Argentine literary culture. He helped to found a literary magazine

Prisma, an Ultraist magazine that only produced two issues and consisted of poems, essays, manifestos, and Norah's woodcut illustrations. The founders of the magazine decorated the city with these issues, pasting them onto walls. After *Prisma*, Borges turned his energies to a new magazine called *Proa*. Although Macedonio Fernández contributed to the magazine, Borges oversaw most of the editing and production. Three editions were published between August 1922 and July 1923, before the journal folded. Borges also published his own work in the magazines *Nosotros* and *Inicial*.

Borges, extremely enthusiastic about Argentina's literary world, published his first book of poems and fell in love with Concepción Guerrero, a woman he'd met at an Ultraist gathering. *Fervor de Buenos Aires*, published in 1923, expresses Borges's love for Concepción as well as for Buenos Aires: "Georgie was writing furiously, and the muse behind the poems that made up his first published volume, *Fervor*, was Concepción," suggests Woodall, "or, perhaps more correctly, Buenos Aires as reflected, through Georgie's imagination, in his beloved" (Woodall 57). Most of the forty-six poems concerned the forgotten parts of the city, the slums and towns on the city's outskirts, quarters that were beginning to disappear in the postwar boom. These parts of the city interested Borges far more than the prosperous downtown. By turning to the subject of Argentina, Borges explored his own heritage and identity.

His father financed the publication of the book, with the front cover displaying one of Norah's woodcuts, and Borges freely distributed almost all 300 copies. The editor of *Nosotros*, Alfredo Bianchi, agreed to help distribute the copies—whenever someone of importance came into his office, he surreptitiously slipped a copy in the pocket of the person's overcoat. The free-verse poems, flavored by local speech and subjects, demonstrated a quiet restraint and began to win Borges recognition.

Just as Borges began to settle into the Buenos Aires literary scene, the family decided to return to Europe so that Jorge could undergo another eye surgery. Although Borges was certainly old enough to stay behind, he chose to follow his family. The Borgeses stayed in Geneva until the summer, and then they went to Spain. While in Spain, Norah spent time with her admirer Guillermo de Torre, a fellow Ultraist who had once co-written a few texts with her brother, and Borges reconnected with Cansinos-Assens. Also during the stay, *Fervor* received a positive review in the Spanish journal *Revista de Occidente*, helping to further establish Borges's reputation. He continued to write articles and lead an active social life. However, disappointed to see that the Ultraist movement was dying out in Spain, he longed to return to Argentina, where he had discovered his true identity as a poet.

As soon as he returned to Buenos Aires, Borges connected with a new set of literary friends. He broke off the engagement with Concepción, and devoted his energy to founding and contributing to magazines. He contributed steadily to *Martin Fierro*, a literary magazine which became a format for anti-establishment writers to express their views. It also served as a platform for the two different Argentine literary groups of which a novelist, Roberto Mariani, announced the existence. The Boedo group represented working-class writers that focused on realism and rough, *gaucho* texts; the Florida group stood for the authors influenced by Europe and the avant-garde. Borges was placed in the latter group; however, he felt he belonged in the former, as his writing concerned the Argentine slums and their local color. While some of the writers took the labels seriously, Borges did not truly care—he was too occupied with launching the rebirth of *Proa*.

In 1924 he teamed with the poet Ricardo Güiraldes, as well as novelist Pablo Rojas Paz, and poet Alfredo Brandán Caraffa, to create a new version of *Proa*. Like Cansinos-Assens and Fernández, Güiraldes, who was older than Borges, left a deep impression on him; during this period of his life, Borges, always eager to feed his intellect, expressed an interest in learning from mentors. After the new *Proa* shut down in 1926, Borges became involved in the journal *Martín Fierro*. When it closed in 1927, he had discovered another mentor—the Mexican writer Alfonso Reyes, who arrived in Buenos Aires as an ambassador. Borges admired Reyes's work, and from him, he learned the power of simplicity and direct writing. He began to dismiss his early writings as youthful and heavily baroque in their style. Borges's enthusiasm for ideas and reading matched his feelings toward nurturing friendships, many of which would last throughout his lifetime.

Between 1925 and 1926 he published a second book of poems called *Luna de enfrente* (*Moon Across the Way*), and two collections of essays: *Inquisiciones* and *El tamano di mi esperanza* (*The Size of My Hope*). *The Size of My Hope* depicted Borges's interest in Jewish culture, and his broad knowledge of Jewish folklore, literature, and mysticism. In these works Borges was also attempting to divorce himself from the image that had been created for him, the one of the European intellectual. Borges lost interest in Ultraism; he now turned to *criollismo*, in which he shunned his Spanish heritage, and connected himself to the "Creole," or native Argentine. Borges explored less reputable areas of the city, learning to tango and talking with hoodlums, all to his mother's dismay, and wrote poems that praised the local traits.

In his romantic life, Borges fell for a seventeen year old named Elsa Astete Millán, who he met through a friend. Borges began to think about marriage; however, over time, whenever he called Elsa, she refused to answer the phone. Finally, he asked her mother why she would not speak with him, and she informed him that Elsa was to be married to someone else. It would be many years before he saw her again.

Borges had more experience with friends than he did with romance. During this time he was friends with many outlandish artists and writers, one of whom was Alejandro Schulz Solari, who went by the pseudonym of Xul Solar. Xul Solar, half-Lithuanian and half-Italian, was an abstract artist sometimes compared to the artist Paul Klee. Xul Solar painted magical supernatural landscapes, and expressed interest in mathematics, astrology, and the Kabbalah. He influenced Borges in his original way of perceiving the world, with its possibilities concerning time, space, and reality. Borges was also friends with the writer Carlos Mastronardi, another eccentric figure who joined Borges on night walks through the city. Mastronardi spent half his life working on a long poem that went largely unread.

In 1928, Borges had to say good-bye to his closest childhood friend. His sister Norah, who had been his best friend during childhood, married Guillermo de Torre and moved to Spain. Unfortunately, in their later years, Borges and Norah would lose their closeness, and toward the end of Borges's life, their relations became strained and unpleasant.

That same year, for the first time, Borges became more directly involved with Argentine politics. In 1928, the seventy-three-year-old Hipólito Irigoyen, a member of the Radical party, hoped to return to the Presidency. Borges held a meeting at his house for artists and poets to pledge their support for his victory. Although Irigoyen won, he would prove to be out of touch with the times, causing Borges to distance himself again from politics.

A year later Borges published another book of poems, *Cuaderno San Martín*, its focus on Palermo, and a book of essays, *El idioma de los argentinos* (*The Language of the Argentines*). He won the Second Municipal Prize of 3000 pesos, and used the money to purchase a complete set of Encyclopedia Britannica. Borges had developed a special affinity for encyclopedias; he had been fascinated by them since he was a child, and throughout his life, turned to them frequently for reading material.

After his family moved once more to another neighborhood of Buenos Aires, Borges focused on writing a longer prose piece. He decided to write a biography on one of his earliest influences, the poet Evaristo Carriego from Palermo who had died of tuberculosis in 1912. The book, *Evaristo Carriego*, more of a reminiscence of old time Buenos Aires than a biography, did not sell well. The majority of Borges's readers happened to be his close friends. However, it was the only book of prose during this era that Borges allowed to remain in print. Later, he would dismiss this period of his career, characterizing his prose as youthful and overly drenched in local color. *The Size of My Hope, The Language of the Argentines,* and *Inquisiciones* were three books he never allowed reprinted, and whenever he noticed the books on friends' shelves, he would ask for permission to destroy their copies.

Dark Times

During the 1930's Borges met three people who significantly impacted his writing career. The first was Victoria Ocampo, whom he had first met in 1925 when he was still editing *Proa*. Ocampo would be his most important professional contact throughout the thirties. Ocampo, nine years older than Borges, was wealthy, intellectual, and outgoing, and expressed an unwavering love for literature. She challenged Borges's rather prim and conservative ideas about women, and described him as "a young man ... with a certain shyness apparent in the way he walked, in his voice, in his handshake and his eyes of *voyant*" (Woodall 84). Raised in an aristocratic family that valued the ways of the French, Victoria launched a literary and intellectual magazine, *Sur*, in 1931, that swayed under an undeniably European influence. *Sur* showcased the best of contemporary writing. Writers including André Gide, Aldous Huxley, Alfonso Reyes, and Borges all appeared in its pages, and in one issue Picasso contributed illustrations.

Borges also met Néstor Ibarra during this period. Ibarra, from France, moved to Buenos Aires in the mid-1920's to complete his university studies. Ibarra was fascinated by Borges's poetry, and the two struck up a friendship that seemed to center around their mutual delight in word games and their appetite for taking night walks around the city. In the 1940's, Ibarra would be important for translating Borges's work into French, helping Borges gain international recognition.

The third person of importance Borges met during this period was the writer Aldofo Bioy Casares, simply called Bioy. Borges first met Bioy in 1932 at one of Ocampo's gatherings. (A few years later, Bioy would marry Victoria's younger sister, Silvina, a painter). Bioy, at seventeen, was well-read, precocious, eager to establish a writing career, and an admirer of Borges's work. The two shared a love for English writers, spending many evenings together dining and discussing literature. As the two could not have looked or acted any more different from each other, they certainly must have turned a few heads: "Bioy was young, elegant, sporty (he loved tennis), and a burgeoning ladies' man" whereas Borges, then thirty-three years old, "was prematurely middle-aged, awkward, physically inept, indifferent to fashion and timid in company" (Woodall 89). Yet the two men established a friendship and literary partnership that lasted a lifetime.

Borges's writing style changed significantly during this time. He did not want to commit himself to a particular style or movement, and slowly began to discover his own individual style of writing. He abandoned the ideas of Ultraism and *criollismo*, and he focused more on prose than poetry. He published an essay in *Sur* in which he was beginning to question realism and to embrace something more fantastic. Borges was moving in a direction different from the other writers of his time. One of the first to completely abandon Modernism, Borges embraced metaphysics, philosophy, and the fantastical, and his style began to develop into something wholly original.

Borges was also beginning to receive more recognition for his writing. In 1932 he published *Discusción*, a collection of essays that reflected his wide range of taste in literature, as well as his love for the cinema. Borges sometimes reviewed films, and later, in interviews, listed his favorites as Hitchcock, American westerns, and musicals—especially *My Fair Lady* and *West Side Story*. In 1933, the journal *Megáfono* devoted a single issue to Borges's work, also bringing him more wide-spread exposure, and Borges published his first short story, called "Streetcorner Man" in *Crítica*, a popular newspaper where Borges was working part-time as an editor of the literary supplement. The story concerns a knife-fight, and the author's byline reads "Francisco Bustos," the name of Borges's great-great grandfather. Borges claimed he used a different name because he knew his mother would not approve of the subject; however, the detail also hints to Borges's developing style, in which hoaxes, disguises, and duplications of identity often appear.

From August 1933 to January 1934, *Crítica* published six of eight pieces that compromised *Historia universal de la infamia (A Universal History of Infamy)*. For this book, Borges took characters and ideas from other published works and recreated them in a series of sketches. The pieces are humorous, playful, and often violent. Blending fact and fiction, often mythic or surrealistic in tone, the stories suggested the direction Borges was about to embark upon in his writing.

During this productive period, Borges met two premier poets, Pablo Neruda and Federico García Lorca. While later in their lives Neruda and Borges would grudgingly acknowledge a respect for each other's work, they never developed a friendship. Politically, they were incompatible, as Neruda joined the Communist Party and Borges abhorred and feared communism throughout his life, especially in his later years. His respect for Neruda did not extend, however, to the Spanish lyric poet Lorca. Part of Borges's dislike for Lorca may have stemmed from jealousy, suggests Woodall, as Lorca was at the height of his fame and Borges was still fairly unsuccessful. Borges often stereotyped Spaniards as "slick and superficial," and he quickly characterized Lorca in this manner (Woodall 98). However, Borges's criticism of Lorca never wavered, even after his tragic death. Years later in a 1968 interview Borges explained that he considered him "a minor poet" (Burgin 69).

Borges published his first piece of "hoax" fiction called "The Approach to al-Mu'tasim," a story disguised as a book review of a fictional novel. Apparently, the hoax worked so well that Bioy tried to order a copy of the imaginary book. This story, a prototype for later fiction, is often considered the first true "Borgesian" story. It appeared in his next published collection of essays, most of them concerning time and metaphysics, called *Historia de al eternidad (History of Eternity)*. Borges claimed this book sold only 37 copies, and years later in an interview he thanked and apologized to the 37 people who purchased it.

Although everything seemed to be falling into place for Borges, he was actually struggling with a dark depression. His friend Bioy described Borges as happy on the outside, but "with what he called a *fondo de tristeza*, a base of sadness, on the inside" (Woodall 96). Scholars have speculated that during this period Borges seriously considered suicide. Although this speculation cannot be confirmed, his sadness was quite real and most likely stemmed from a combination of issues: the political climate, personal problems, and the gloom at home.

Borges wrote steadily in a climate that was gradually darkening, both figuratively and literally. The world had plunged into economic crises. Although Argentina seemed far away from these troubles, the country was anxious, and underwent several changes in leadership. A right-wing coup had ousted President Irigoyen in 1930, and the conservative government of President Uriburu took over. In turn, Uriburu's regime was forced out by General Agustin Justo in late 1931. Justo managed to stay in office seven years, until Roberto Ortiz came into power in 1938. During all of the political turmoil, locally and globally, Borges was one of the few in Argentina to denounce the trend toward anti-Semitism. The political climate grew more unbearable for Borges with every passing year. Argentina remained politically neutral during most of the war; however, Borges feared what he believed was a growing wave of fascism. When war broke out in Europe in 1939, Nationalism was at the forefront in Argentina. Borges distanced himself from Nationalism and embraced pro-Europe views, which he would espouse for the rest of his life. Borges, his friends, and *Sur* were in the minority in their support for the Allies. With the outbreak of a Civil War in Spain, *Sur* published many poems expressing outrage at the murder of Lorca, killed by Granada Fascists.

On a more private sphere, Borges battled a literal darkness, as the congenital eye defect that had affected his father and grandmother also began to take its inevitable toll on him. He underwent his first operation for cataracts in 1927, the first of many operations.

However, the physical problems did not seem to him to be as terrifying as his loneliness. In his mid-thirties, Borges was chubby and socially awkward, especially around women. The women he came into contact with were usually rich, sophisticated, and beautiful, a contrast to Borges who was poor and shy. He had experienced very little intimacy or romance in his life. He struggled with endless insomnia during this period, and depended upon his mother to look after his needs.

When he was not spending time writing or with friends, he was usually at home with his family, further agitating his sadness. In 1935 his beloved grandmother Fanny died at ninety-three years old. Meanwhile, the health of his father continued to fail. The elder Jorge was now completely blind, "a sad, unfulfilled figure, who sat for hours in silence, staring into nothingness" (Woodall 104).

Financial troubles also plagued Borges. His books did not sell well, and although he took a couple of different editing jobs and contributed to *Sur*, these positions paid very little, if at all. It was becoming more difficult for the family to survive on Jorge's pension.

Finally, at thirty-eight years old, Borges accepted his first full-time job as the First Assistant at the Miguel Cané branch of the Municipal Library, a job that involved classifying and cataloguing the library's small collection. Borges later said that there were fifty-some employees, whereas fifteen would have sufficed. When he first started the job, his colleagues told him he was working too fast and they warned him to slow down, so that they could spread out the task for as long as possible. Finding the job boring and repetitive, Borges described the position as nine years of "solid unhappiness." His colleagues, more interested in women and horse-racing than in literature, did not even recognize their co-worker as the author of the books they catalogued. The library was unsafe and violent—once a woman was raped on her way to the bathroom—and overall, a miserable place to work.

The only benefit was that Borges always found time to write. After easily finishing his menial tasks, he often spent the rest of the hours in the library's basement, writing, reading, or translating fiction (Borges was the first to translate the works of Virginia Woolf and William Faulkner into Spanish). Borges wrote furiously and continued to educate himself through reading. The long ride on the train to and from work provided him with plenty of time to read. Once he read an English-Italian version of Dante's *Divine Comedy* on the train. He would read a page in English, then study the lines in Italian, and somewhere in the midst of the book, he realized he had taught himself Italian.

Then, in 1938, two tragic events took place. First, his father died on February 24, a few months after Borges had started his job at the library. This loss took a heavy toll on Borges. Before he died, his father made a wish that Borges rewrite his only novel, to improve it. It was a task Borges never undertook, and later regretted that he had not fulfilled his father's wish.

Then on Christmas Eve of the same year, a strange accident occurred. Borges was running up the dark stairway to an apartment when he hit the glass door. The glass shattered, bits of it lodged into his head, and soon the wound was infected and he underwent an operation for blood-poisoning. For a month Borges hovered between life and death, hallucinating and wild with fever. His mother cared for him, reading aloud C.S. Lewis's *Out of the Silent Planet*. Borges, on hearing the words, wept with understanding. Although Leonor's and Borges's description of the accident never quite matched and many details were left unexplained, it was an impetus for the next stage of Borges's career.

Fictive Reality

Borges feared that in this period of hovering between life and death, his creative impulses had been destroyed. He would never be more wrong: on recovery, Borges burned with a creative energy that eventually would lead him to international recognition and fame. The accident symbolized an important break in his career: he now turned his attention to fiction. He explained the shift in a 1966 interview:

> I began to fear for my mental integrity—I said, 'Maybe I can't write anymore.' Then my life would have been practically over because literature is very important to me. Not because I think my own stuff particularly good, but because I know that I can't get alone without writing. If I don't write, I feel, well, a kind of remorse, no? Then I thought I would try my hand at writing an article or a poem. But I thought: I have written hundreds of articles and poems. If I can't do it, then I'll know at once that I am done for, that everything is over with me. So I thought I'd try my hand at something I hadn't done: If I couldn't do it, there would be nothing strange about it because why should I write short stories?—It would prepare me for the final overwhelming blow: knowing that I was at the end of my tether. (Christ 117)

What Borges discovered was that he was at the beginning of a productive period for writing short stories. After the accident, Borges wrote two stories that ignited his career. "Pierre Menard, Author of the *Quixote*" and "Tlön, Uqbar, Orbis Tertius" appeared a year apart in *Sur*. Both stories perplexed their readers, offering complex critiques of realism and posing questions of identity (for example, Borges and his friends appear as characters, blurring the lines between what is real and imaginary). These stories marked the beginning of Borges's "ficciones," short non-traditional narratives that would make him famous. Interestingly, Borges never wrote a novel, and much of his publications were short fragments. He liked to joke that he only wrote poems and short pieces because he was "lazy."

The first story, "Pierre Menard," operates as a hoax story that posed as a critical investigation, while "Tlön, Uqbar, Orbis Tertius," even more experimental and strange, concerns the discovery of a fictional country. Woodall attests that the story worked on several levels: "In Tlön, Borges was at one level pursuing a way of depicting the dizzying rift between fact and imagination, truth and its opposite—perhaps indefinable; at another, he was offering a metaphor for global catastrophe" (Woodall 115). Indeed, the world felt as if it were on the brink of chaos. Borges condemned Hitler and the Nazis, as he watched his country become more entrenched in corruption and fascism. Literature provided a platform from which Borges could question the world around him.

When Borges was not busy writing, he was working at the library or spending time with friends and family. Norah and Guillermo de Torre had returned from Paris, where they had been living since the failure of Republican Spain, and the family lived together for a short time until Borges and his mother moved to a separate flat.

Through 1940–41, he wrote the rest of stories that became *El jardín de senderos que se bifurcan* (*The Garden of Forking Paths*). The stories break down traditional genre boundaries and use complex narrative techniques. For example, a story that on first glance appeared to be a simple detective story typically turned into a labyrinth of ideas. One of the stories in this collection is "The Library of Babel," a frightening allegory that detailed his job at the library. The stories—complex, philosophical, fantastical, and multi-layered—depict Borges's growing fascination with metaphysics, ancient Gnostics, and mathematical notions. Many readers found the stories strange, including his own mother, who worried about her son's dark imagination.

His friend Bioy clearly understood Borges's genius and greatly admired his work. In turn, Borges felt strongly about Bioy's work, and he wrote a praising foreword to Bioy's most famous novel, *The Invention of Morel*. Their influence over each other was mutual. For example, Borges admitted that the younger writer led him toward classicism, a writing style that showed restraint. Bioy and Borges also shared an appreciation for parody and jokes. In 1942 they published a series of spoof detective stories called *Six Problems for Don Isidro Parodi*, stories full of erudite jokes and confusing plots that mocked the literary establishment. The detective stories represented a humorous game for them, and they laughed and joked while they composed them. Borges later commented that the collaboration allowed them to create another identity: "So we have created between us a kind of third person; we have somehow begotten a third person that is quite unlike us" (Christ 133).

Because of the political climate of Argentina, which was steeped in Nationalism, *The Garden of Forking Paths* was overlooked for a national prize. An anonymous critique from someone in the National Commission for Culture singled out Borges's "English tendencies." *Sur* responded to the insult by devoting an entire issue to Borges.

Borges was not a political writer, but some of his work responded to the precarious political climate, albeit on a symbolic or allegorical level. For example, in *Poemas (1922–1943)*, his first book of poetry since 1929, the poem "Conjectural Poem" speaks to the power of Juan Domingo Perón. The current political climate in Argentina deeply troubled Borges. When Paris was liberated, Borges felt "a *physical* happiness" and many gathered to celebrate the liberation (qtd. in Woodall 129). The military violently dispersed the crowd, and although Borges did not attend the celebration, the event signaled to him a telling sign of the brewing oppressive atmosphere. Instability continued its trend: President Ortiz was replaced by the corrupt Castillo, and Castillo was ousted by the army. General Pedro Ramírez was installed, until he was dismissed in 1944, after he agreed to the U.S. to cut off all diplomatic ties with the Axis. Another general, Edelmiro Farrell, took his place. The military was essentially running the country; political parties were abolished and military propaganda abounded.

Meanwhile, Colonel Juan Domingo Perón became vice-president, and was in the process of wooing Argentines in this precarious and divisive atmosphere. His promotion of workers' rights, anti-imperialism, economic independence, and military security spoke to the population. In addition, a popular wave of an anti-imperialist (anti-British) attitude helped bring Perón to power. Woodall explains that "his big smile, his radio-friendly voice, his slicked-back black hair, and not least of all his blond mistress, Eva Duarte" offered "the charismatic possibility of achieving a new order without bloodshed or corruption" (Woodall 133). However, Borges despised Perón, considering him a "gaucho"—and not in a romanticized way. Borges denounced Perón as power-hungry, aggressive, and offensive. He believed Perón stood for Fascism and was appalled by his rising popularity; Borges was convinced that the Argentine people were being duped.

MARRIAGE PROPOSAL

In 1944, when he was forty-five years old, Borges met Estela Canto. Estela was financially independent, intelligent, and politically astute, and Borges was immediately attracted to her. They spent time together, dining and taking long rambling walks. They talked about literature and politics. Both of them despised Perón, but their tastes in literature differed. When Estela told him Bernard Shaw was her favorite writer, Borges responded that she was the first woman he had ever met who liked Shaw. Estela admired Shaw's rebelliousness, and this surprised Borges, who continued to have outdated, conservative views toward women. In response, Canto disliked what she considered Borges's rigid and male-dominated tastes in literature (the only woman writer on his bookshelves was the poet Emily Dickinson).

Although she was not physically drawn to him, Estela enjoyed her talks with Borges: "Everything Borges said had a magical quality. Like a conjuror, he pulled unexpected objects out of an inexhaustible hat.... And they were magical because they suggest the man he really was, the man hidden behind the Georgie whom we knew, a man who, in his shyness, was struggling to emerge, to be recognized" (qtd. in Woodall 139). Estela considered Borges the leading literary intellectual of Buenos Aires. He was certainly on the beginning path of reaching international recognition. His work was translated into French by Ibarra and Roger Caillois, who promoted Borges throughout Europe. Meanwhile, Borges struck up an important relationship with the publishing house Emecé. They published his prose and his translations of James, Melville, Kafka, and Faulkner. Then, when his collection of stories *Ficciones* was published in 1944, Sociedad Argentina de Escritoreas (Argentina Society for Writers) granted Borges a Grand Honorary Prize.

However, unlike his writing career, his personal life was troubled and complicated. After spending many evenings together, Borges worked up the nerve to propose to Estela. Surprised, she swiftly responded, "I would do it, Georgie, but you mustn't forget I'm a disciple of Bernard Shaw. We can't get married if we haven't already slept together" (qtd. in Woodall 145). Borges was confused and dismayed by her response. According to Woodall, Borges was "paralyzed" sexually, terrified of sexual relations (140). Although the reasons were complicated and impossible to fully understand, part of his fear stemmed from the alienation he experienced with his own physical body. He was also deeply affected by his initial introduction to women, when his father had arranged for him to meet with a prostitute in Switzerland. Regardless of the source of the problem, it was clear to most that Borges battled with profound sexual anxieties.

Borges's physical relationship with Estela never moved beyond kissing. Although the two continued to see each other even after she turned down his marriage proposal, the relationship grew more complicated. One issue concerned Borges's mother. Leonor did not approve of Estela. Similarly, Estela did not like Borges's mother, causing much friction and desperation for Borges. Woodall suggests that Leonor's strong presence in her son's life bothered Estela: "Estela felt deeply uncomfortable about the idea of agreeing to marry a man who would have to ask his mother's permission to do so" (Woodall 146).

The volatile political atmosphere also affected their relationship. Police vigilance tightened, and twice the couple was arrested for not having their papers. Borges was angry and humiliated, and Estela, who despised the political climate just as much as Borges, planned to leave Buenos Aires. They spent less and less time together.

Then, in February 1946, Perón was elected President. Curiously, right after Perón's election, Borges lost his position at the library and was "promoted" to inspector of poultry and rabbits. Although Borges always believed Perón was personally responsible, others assumed it had been the prank of an intellectual involved in the Peronist movement. Borges openly denounced Perón in the next issue of *Sur*, arguing that the dictatorship would only foster oppression. For the rest of his life, Borges assailed Perón.

Borges quickly resigned from the library; he was forty-seven years old. Although he had taken an editing job at a new journal, *Anales de Buenos Aries*, and still contributed to *Sur*, his financial earnings were quite limited. He found himself in a desperate situation: he had lost his job, his relationship with Estela was over, and the dreaded Perón was President. Borges needed some sort of help, and this arrived in the form of a psychiatrist. Woodall suspects the sessions centered on Borges's sexual problems. Whatever the topics in these private meetings, the sessions seemed to work. During the fifties Borges apparently engaged in sexual relations with a dancer, and the sessions also seemed to light his creative fire.

During the next year Borges published five more stories. He and his mother moved to a flat right at the edge of Buenos Aires' commercial center. Then Borges was offered a job to teach English literature at the Argentine Association for English Culture; nearly simultaneously, the Free College for Higher Studies asked him to give a series of lectures on American writers. The idea of lecturing filled Borges with dread. He had tried to give a lecture the year before in Montevideo; however, public speaking terrified him, and he ended up stuttering and stammering so noticeably that someone else actually delivered the lecture for him. Yet, Borges eventually overcame this fear (the sessions with the psychiatrist were a factor in his cure); lecturing would become one of his mainstays for the rest of his life and often provided him with opportunities to travel. He lectured on a wide range of subjects, including Buddhism, Blake, gauchesco poetry, the Kabbalah, and Cervantes.

To prepare, he wrote out notes, committed the lectures to memory, and often practiced by lecturing to Leonor. One of his biographers, Emir Rodríguez Monegal, knew Borges during this time and described one of his lectures: "Borges sat very quietly, never looking directly at the audience and focusing his half-blind eyes on a distant spot. While lecturing, he would join his hands in small, precise movements of prayer or discreetly move them around; he would deliver his speech in a rather monotonous, low voice as if he were a priest or rabbi" (Monegal 395). Borges's voice was quite low, and as he aged, he became more difficult to hear. His rapt audience listened carefully to his words.

The collection of stories, *El Aleph*, published in 1949, was one of his most famous publications, receiving both popular and critical response. The subjects of the thirteen stories include gauchos, death, time, contradictory universes, metaphysics, and conundrums.

Despite these new positive circumstances in his life, his feelings about Perón did not abate and only intensified when his mother and sister were arrested at an anti-Perón rally. Leonor was sentenced to house arrest; Norah spent a month in jail.

The following year Borges was elected President of SADE (Sociedad Argentina de Escritores). The organization, more political than literary, was anti-Peronist. Government officials and police watched over the meetings, so the group would often discuss complex philosophical or literary ideas, until the officials fell asleep or were bored and no longer paying attention—then the true political conversations would take place. After his mother and sister were arrested, the police and government officials often shadowed Borges, following him on his evening walks, or showing up to his lectures. Perón eventually closed SADE; however, after his fall from power in 1955, the organization eventually reopened.

In the 1950s, after the publication of *El Aleph*, Borges participated in many collaborations. Over his lifetime, Borges co-authored and edited numerous books. Most of his collaborators were with women. He collaborated on books about a wide range of subjects, including gauchesco poetry, fantastical literature, and European literature. He also continued to collaborate with Bioy on their detective books.

Several other publishing events occurred during the early fifties, elevating Borges' status and fame. In 1951, Emecé published *La muerte y la brújula*, which consisted of nine stories from *Ficciones* and *El Aleph*. Then, *Ficciones* and a new collection called *Labyrinths*, which contained only four stories, were translated into French. The French consistently lauded Borges throughout his career. In Argentina, two earlier essay collections were republished, and a new collection, *Other Inquisitions*, appeared in 1952. These thirty-nine essays were drawn from fifteen years of critical writing, and included topics such as Borges' favorite writers, as well as his philosophical musings on time and existence.

Although the late forties and early fifties were rich in publications for Borges, he would never again write any more fiction that matched the superior work of *El Aleph*.

A Return to Poetry

The economy in collapse, Perón's dictatorship ended in 1955 and he was exiled to Spain. When the military took over, Borges praised the replacement—in his eyes, anything was progress over Perón. Borges continued to speak out against Perón, refusing to acknowledge any improvements the Perón administration made concerning social issues. Eventually, these views would bring Borges much unwanted attention.

Coincidentally, with the end of Perón's rule, Borges found himself presented with many new opportunities. He accepted the position of Professor of English and American Literature at the Faculty of Philosophy and Letters at Buenos Aires University, a post he held until 1968. He also returned to the library—not the municipal library, but the new government offered Borges a post he could not refuse: Director of the National Library. Borges remained in this honorable position for eighteen years. Although the nominal position did not require much work, Borges enjoyed spending his days at the office in the grand building and showed up nearly every day. He also helped in turning the library into a cultural center, starting a program of lectures and resurrecting the library's journal.

Borges felt at home in the library, surrounded by his first true love—books. By this time, Borges's vision had worsened, and he was nearly blind. The vision in his left eye was completely gone, and he only possessed a blur of vision in his right. The operations for cataracts started in 1927; by the mid-fifties, he had undergone eight operations. He wrote about the experience of working in a library while blind in a poem called "Poem of the Gifts" and referred to the irony in a 1968 interview, commenting that he was surrounded by "800,000 volumes of the National Library and I have been getting closer to darkness ever since that time" (Burgin 43).

The decline of his eyesight progressed steadily over the next decade. Borges explained the inevitable development: "There was a moment where I could only read the title page or the words on the spine, and then another when I could read nothing at all" (Burgin 43).

The last color that he saw was yellow, "the most vivid of colors" (Christ 120). Borges adjusted to this darkness by arranging the books he routinely consulted, such as dictionaries, or books on theology and philosophy, in a particular order—they filled his large, ornate office at the library, and he knew how to locate them by position and size. In his biography, Monegal describes Borges leading him through the library:

> Borges took me in hand and led me around, seeing only enough to know where each book he wanted was. He can open a book to the desired page and, without bothering to read ... quote complete passages. He roams along corridors lined with books; he quickly turns corners and gets into passages which are truly invisible, mere cracks in the walls of books; he rushes down winding staircases which abruptly end in the dark. (Monegal 431)

Borges's excellent sense of memory and direction allowed him to navigate both physical and mental spaces. Even nearing blindness, Borges continued to take walks around the city. When he was with an interviewer or friend, he often grabbed the person's arm with a strong grip, and led the person around in an almost brusque manner.

Borges had never learned to type; he always wrote using a pen, in spidery, minuscule letters. Although losing their eyesight would likely devastate most writers, Borges knew the blindness was inevitable, and he was prepared to alter his writing process in order to continue working. Just like his father had before him, Borges depended entirely on his mother for survival—she cared for him, read to him, and now that he could no longer write, took notes and dictation. For the rest of his life, Borges wrote by dictating all of his work. He learned to become an oral writer.

Whenever he was at home, his mother fulfilled this position of secretary, but at his office at the library, where he went daily, nearly anyone who stopped by could find themselves in the position of taking dictation. Usually, just like his collaborators, they were young women. Borges worked carefully and slowly, and he was always apologetic about the time commitment. He would dictate a verse of poetry, then immediately ask for the verse to be read aloud. This would continue over and over, until after two or three hours, he would have a poem or half a page of prose, although the former was more likely.

With his blindness, Borges had changed not only his writing process, but also the form in which he wrote. He now composed predominantly poetry: "A return to poetry was the most significant shift of literary emphasis Borges had made since sitting down to write "Pierre Menard" (Woodall 181). Borges had started his career as a poet, and now, in his mid-fifties, he was returning to this form. From 1964–85, Borges published eight volumes of poetry.

The most significant reason for returning to poetry was that, unlike prose, poetry was a form he could "see" in his head. Sonnets, specifically, were a formal structure which he could memorize and then compose. On his walks around the library or along the streets, he wrote them in his mind, claiming that a sonnet had "mnemonic value" and was "a portable thing." He further explained: "I can go on walking all over the town while I carry a sonnet in my head, polishing and altering as I go. You can't do that with a long piece of prose" (Burgin 44).

When he was not busy writing, teaching, or lecturing, Borges engaged in another intellectual activity—learning Anglo-Saxon and Old Norse. He originally met with a group of interested students with the idea of exploring literature outside the curriculum; these meetings developed into an Anglo-Saxon and Old Norse study group. He ignored Leonor's suggestion to try Greek instead; Borges knew that his understanding of the German language and etymology would allow him to grasp some of the roots of Old English. Borges did not lecture to the students; instead, it was a collaborative effort to teach themselves. They would consult dictionaries and read aloud, and together, try to figure out the meanings and pronunciations. The study group served as a hobby for Borges, and fulfilled his passion for the studying of language and etymology. This new pastime also stimulated his memory, and fostered his romantic feelings for the old country, England.

By the mid-fifties, Borges received more prestigious recognition, along with numerous honors. He received an honorary doctorate degree from Cuyo, one of Argentina's oldest universities, and he won the National Prize for literature. Scholarly books about his life and work appeared, and he was rapidly attracting a wide circle of devoted students. Most of the critics praised Borges, although a few viewed him as elitist—a perspective which often grew out of observing his conservative politics and devotion to Europe.

In 1960 he published *El hacedor* (*Dreamtigers*), a book comprised of scenes, vignettes, literary montages, parables, and poems. The most famous piece in the book is the last entry, "Borges and I," in which he ironically claims that Borges is a separate person: "It's to the other man, to Borges, that things happen.... I live, I let myself live, so that Borges can weave his tales and poems, and those tales and poems are my justification." Always experimenting with changes in identity, now Borges had created a Borges persona: "In the most cunning and diverting move of his literary career, Borges had become his double" (Woodall 190). This "other" Borges was not shy or awkward; this was the Borges who wrote, traveled, often exaggerated, and performed. In a 1982 interview Borges aptly described the dual identity:

> As for two Borges, I have been made keenly aware of the fact that there are two, because when I think of myself, I think, let us say, of a rather secret, of a rather hesitant, groping man. Somehow, this can hardly be reconciled to the fact that I seem to be giving lectures all the time and traveling all over the world. So I think of those two men as being different: the private man and the public man. (Burgin 197)

Often in interviews, Borges, always full of wit, would refer to this other, and talked about himself in the third-person, and the interviewers participated in the game, asking Borges about "Borges." The reporters helped to create Borges as a shadowy figure, so that at times people even wondered if he was more than one persona, which only delighted Borges.

International Recognition

Although Borges was translated into French in the 1940s, offering him a glimpse of international recognition, it was not until 1961 that he began to gain world-wide fame. This was the year that he won the Formentor Prize, an international award of $10,000, created by six international publishers. The publishers split the award between Borges and the French writer Samuel Beckett. Although the sum of money was impressive, it did not compare to the immediate prestige that the prize provided Borges. The award shone a global spotlight over him: "Borges became a fêted literary personality almost overnight. For major literary cultures ... it was as if he alone had altered the way people wrote and thought about writing" (Woodall 194). His work was translated into English, and *Ficcones*, the first Latin American work to receive such international attention, was translated into several languages.

That same year the University of Texas in Austin invited Borges to serve a post that required lectures and readings, and Borges, accompanied by his mother, made his first trip to the United States. Borges caused a stir for the American academic world: an exciting writer of international claim, Borges broke down boundaries with his work. His experimental fiction was a welcomed change from the realism and academic writing that dominated American fiction.

Borges's influence over both American and Latin American writers is undeniable. Although he never wrote a novel, his work paved the way for many of the great present-day novelists. In Latin America, he made an indelible impression on authors such as Julio Cortázar and Gabriel García Márquez. In a famous quote, the novelist Carlos Fuentes claimed that without Borges's prose "the modern Latin Novel would not exist" (qtd. in Bell-Villada 45). As Borges's work opened a space for many new possibilities, such as magic realism and experimentation, he was also praised for his controlled and precise language. Although his influence over Latin America literature was unquestionable, his political leanings often caused rifts with his overall reception in Argentina. He was actually more well received in the United States.

Borges's writing had a powerful effect on American writers. His work influenced such postmodern writers as Thomas Pynchon, Robert Coover, Donald Barthelme, and John Barth. His personality also left a positive impression on his admirers, and the American universities welcomed his visits. His combination of conservative dress, courteous manners, and sharp wit intrigued his audiences. He was perceived as an exotic figure, "unseeing, nannied, professionally, vastly lettered, talkative, and perfectly comfortable with his fame" (Woodall 197). Borges's lectures were often more like intellectually playful chats than traditional lectures, and his appearance and presentation were popular with university audiences. "Having apparently turned modern fiction inside-out," surmises Woodall, "here was a besuited blind man delighting his audiences with runic word-play, and making metaphysical jokes about Milton" (196).

Before returning to Buenos Aires, Borges and Leonor (who were often mistaken as brother and sister, or husband and wife), traveled around the country, including visits to New York, New Mexico, and Massachusetts. Borges greatly enjoyed the visit, praising the generosity and friendliness of the people he met in the United States.

A flurry of national and international honors followed him on his return, including his election to the Argentine Academy of Letters, and his award of the French government's Commandeur de l'Ordre des Arts et Lettres. He was also featured in *Time* magazine, referred to as perhaps the greatest living writer in the Spanish language.

Then, in 1963, Borges traveled to Europe. The initial impetus for the trip was an invitation from the British Council, but the trip expanded to include invites from Paris and Madrid. It was Borges's first time in Europe since 1924, and the tour allowed him to revisit many locations from his childhood, and meet with old friends and associates. His mother happily accompanied him. Throughout much of Borges's career, Leonor acted as his secretary and constant companion. She traveled with him, managed his personal affairs and finances, took notes and dictation, and read to him. The universities and media adored Leonor nearly as much as they did her famous son: "[Borges] and Leonor were it seemed, a couple surrounded by their own unique *porteño* mythology" (Woodall 213). Leonor, a modern and stylishly attractive woman, was energetic and outgoing. She impressed reporters with her cultivated tastes, speaking both English and French. She had even worked with Borges on several translations, including translations of Virginia Woolf novels.

First they visited Madrid, where Borges met with his former mentor, the eighty-one-year-old Cansinos-Assens. Then mother and son traveled to Geneva and Paris, and ended the trip in England. Borges established a good relationship with the British Council—the members, delighted with Borges, praised his modesty and courtesy.

Although the international recognition swept Borges out of obscurity, providing him with prestige and prosperity, the fame also threatened to negatively affect Borges's life as a writer. For the first time in his career, he was writing infrequently, as other obligations began to take priority over his work.

Companionship

For the next trip Borges made to Europe, he replaced his faithful traveling companion. Leonor was nearly ninety-years-old, and although she thoroughly enjoyed the last trip to Europe, the traveling exhausted her. Borges could not make the voyage alone—he needed a caretaker. Mariá Esther Vazquez, forty years his junior, seemed like the ideal companion. Borges had known Mariá Esther for a few years; she took dictation for him, and often helped him with his work at the library. Vazquez was extremely intelligent and admired Borges's work; there was no reason for her to suspect that Borges had feelings for her that went beyond professional admiration. To Vazquez, Borges seemed "as old as the Pyramids" (qtd. in Woodall 204). But Borges, obviously attracted to Mariá Esther, assumed her feelings were mutual.

The two traveled first to Berlin, where Borges had been invited by the Congress for Cultural Freedom, and followed the visit with to a trip to Stockholm. In Paris Borges lectured on Shakespeare, and spent time with his translator Néstor. He also went to England as a guest of the British Council. Although he was not lecturing in England, the Council members had enjoyed Borges so much that they provided him with funding and resources. The director, Neil MacKay, commented that Borges was "a very childlike person in many ways and it is hard to disappoint him" (qtd. in Woodall 206). Borges and Vazquez finished the tour in Spain.

Back in Buenos Aires, Borges and Mariá Esther collaborated on two projects, a revised book on Germanic literature that Borges had published and an introduction to English literature for Argentine students. Borges believed they had more than merely a professional relationship, but as Woodall points out, he was "strangely incapable of reading the human heart" (204). Also, Borges wanted to be married; he longed for a romantic partner. He began to equate marriage with happiness. Now that he had acquired such international fame, he wanted someone to share the spotlight with him—other than his mother. Part of Borges's desire for marriage also arose from his need for a permanent caretaker. While he adored his mother, she was getting old, and he longed for a young woman companion who would care for him. He believed that with Vazquez, marriage was a possibility.

So when Mariá Esther announced her engagement to someone else, Borges was devastated. Some friends believed Vazquez had strung him along, but it was also entirely possible that a romantic possibility had been Borges's hopeful invention. Regardless, he was deeply saddened. On hearing the wedding announcement, he went to the dentist to have his teeth pulled, as if the physical discomfort could alleviate his emotional pain.

In 1964, he published *Obra poética*, a collection of poems, some of which were taken from *Dreamtigers*, but most of his creative work now arrived in the form of collaborative projects with young women, giving him a respite from his loneliness. The projects provided him a chance for temporary companionship, and also allowed him to exercise his memory and intellect. He also collaborated with Bioy to write another detective story, full of jokes and pranks.

In 1965, Borges went on a trip to lecture in Chile and Colombia, and this time he took an old married friend, signaling the end of his relationship with Mariá Esther. He resigned from his post at the university, most likely because his progressive blindness made teaching too difficult, and survived on a pension and award money. Borges had never placed very much importance on money. His mother always took care of his finances, and Borges, more concerned with literature than riches, had often struggled with minuscule earnings.

On the outside, Borges seemed content. However, his friends knew of his feelings of loneliness. He did not seem to have any romantic interests in his sights, until he saw Elsa Astete Millán once again. She was one of his first loves, a young woman he had first met forty-some years ago and who had married his friend Ricardo Albarracín. Borges had heard that Albarracín had died three years ago of lung cancer, and that Elsa had become reclusive and withdrawn. He had not communicated with her for over twenty years (around the time *Ficciones* was published, he had sent her two letters attesting to his love). Now, he called on the fifty-seven-year old woman, who had a grown son, and embarked on one of the more unusual periods in his life.

On visiting with Elsa, the two talked away the afternoon, and then went to dinner and the movies, renewing their friendship. A few months later, in 1967, they were married.

At first, Leonor did not approve of Elsa, as she seemed too uneducated and uncultured for Borges. But eventually Leonor softened, happy that her son had finally found a wife. To Borges's friends, the couple seemed ill-suited for each other. Elsa, who spoke only Spanish, did not share Borges's intellectual interests, and Borges, who led a life of traveling, writing, and spending time with his friends, was not accustomed to domesticity. For the first time in his life, at sixty-eight years old, Borges moved out of his mother's house. He and Elsa lived together in a flat, sleeping in separate bedrooms.

The year they were married, Borges returned to the United States to accept the Charles Eliot Norton Poetry Chair at Harvard University. Elsa accompanied him, and in the beginning, Borges seemed happy about the marriage. He traveled around New England, met new people, and gave six honorary lectures called "The Craft of Verse." Elsa took care of the household duties and the finances, read to, and took dictation for Borges. It must have been frustrating to move away from her home to a foreign land, where her husband was often away, lecturing and engaging with his friends. However, Elsa eventually adjusted to her husband and this new way of life; it was Borges who had trouble changing his ways.

During his time at Harvard, Borges met Norman Thomas di Giovanni, a thirty-four-year-old Italian-American translator living outside of Boston. He had never heard of Borges, but when he discovered one of his poems while he was working on an anthology, he quickly went out and bought his book. He was thrilled to find out that Borges was lecturing at Harvard. Borges agreed to meet him, and it was the beginning of a very important relationship. For the next few years, di Giovanni would become a good friend, a literary collaborator, and his principal translator.

Back in Buenos Aires, Borges and Elsa settled into a routine: Elsa woke him, prepared his bath and breakfast, and then Borges went to the library. Every evening they dined at the Bioys. Although Borges had found someone other than his mother to take care of him, he and Elsa did not share any common interests. Something was missing for Borges. He was not writing, or traveling, and he felt generally unhappy about the marriage.

The situation felt hopeless, but it was about to change. In November 1968, di Giovanni arrived in Buenos Aires to continue working on Borges's translations. Initially, di Giovanni intended to stay only a few months; however, he would extend the visit to four years.

The Influence of di Giovanni

Borges and di Giovanni embarked on what would be Borges last great and productive period of work. They focused their early attentions on translating Borges's poems. In looking over all of Borges unpublished poems, di Giovanni realized that Borges could publish a new collection if he would write thirteen more new poems. At first, Borges vehemently protested. He was afraid of writing a new book; he had not written anything new in a quite a while, and he did not want to be judged by what he feared was below-standard work. Battling a creative block, Borges felt depressed and creatively drained. However, eventually he began to consider the proposition, especially when his best friend Bioy told him he thought it sounded like a good idea. For the first time since *Dreamtigers*, Borges began to plan another book.

Borges and di Giovanni worked hard. In the mornings Borges dictated to three different secretaries who rotated shifts; in the afternoons he and di Giovanni embarked on the translations. Their level of productivity was remarkable. They started with a translation of *The Book of Imaginary Beings*, adding four new entries, and on Borges's 70th birthday, in 1969, *In Praise of Darkness*—the new book of poems which contained six short prose pieces—was published. Borges and di Giovanni signed a contract to co-translate eight more volumes. Meanwhile, Borges had also started to work on a new short story.

It was not just the publications that were important—it was that Borges had regained his confidence: "Borges the married man had become a writer again" (Woodall 223). Di Giovanni, extroverted, energetic, and ambitious, had a powerful and exciting effect on Borges. In just a year, the difference in Borges's creative output was astounding. With someone by his side who supported and challenged him, Borges remembered what a great and strange writer he was: "In essence what di Giovanni did was to stimulate Borges's imagination, and his memory: he reminded Borges of what narrative powers he had, of what use he could put them to" (Woodall 225).

In 1970, Borges published a collection of eleven new stories called *Doctor Brodie's Report*. These stories take place in Argentina and concern knife-fights and gauchos. While these stories consist of more straightforward narratives than *El Aleph* or *Ficciones*, the collection is still impressive and stirring, with an undercurrent of experimentation rippling through the collection.

After the publication of *In Praise of Darkness*, the University of Oklahoma invited Borges to give six lectures. For the first time, swayed by Di Giovanni's suggestion, Borges, although anxious and nervous about the decision, delivered a lecture that focused on his personal life. Di Giovanni felt that Borges's fans wanted to know more about the mysterious, exotic intellectual writer: "I knew that readers were having difficulty with Borges; worse, I knew that the universities keep him swathed in unnecessary mystery. At the same time, since his stories were really all about himself, his various guises, and dimensions of his thought, what better setting for them by way of introduction than the story of his life?" (qtd. in Woodall 229). When he returned to Buenos Aires, Borges reworked this lecture into what was titled, "Autobiographical Essay," which published in the *New Yorker* for $9,000.

Creatively, Borges seemed unstoppable, but in the spring of 1970, he experienced an emotional breakdown about his personal life, confessing to di Giovanni, "I've committed what seems to me now an unaccountable mistake, a huge mistake. A quite unexplainable and mysterious mistake" (qtd. in Woodall 230). The mistake he was referring to was his marriage. The marriage was a failure, and Borges was anxious to leave its confines. However, instead of trying to talk to Elsa about his concerns, he only consulted di Giovanni, gladly letting him take over to "solve" the problem. Di Giovanni took the necessary recourse for Borges, speaking to a lawyer and arranging the separation (divorce was not legal in Argentina).

Borges never mustered the courage, or found the courtesy, to talk to Elsa. Instead, he planned a day of escape. One morning after breakfast, on his way out of the house, Elsa asked him what he would like for lunch, and he told her, *puchero*, one of his favorite meals. However, that afternoon Borges did not come home for lunch. Instead, five men showed up, two lawyers with a legal order for separation and three movers to take away Borges's belongings.

Meanwhile, Borges was on his way to Córdoba, to lecture and, essentially, hide from the situation. Elsa, as expected, was stunned—not just by the end of the marriage, but by Borges's lack of respect. She later admitted this was "this was the biggest shock of my life" and never forgave Borges for the way he left her (qtd. in Woodall 231). The marriage had lasted less than three years; on his return to Buenos Aires, Borges moved back in with his mother.

The Interviews

With his new-found freedom, Borges continued writing and traveling. He went to Brazil to receive a major biennial Latin American prize called the Inter-American Prize for Literature, worth $25,000. However, he cut the trip short to return home to be with his mother, who had grown frail and sick in the last few years. Borges's cousin Esther Haedo attests that Borges's marriage could have accelerated her old age, that when her son was married, she realized he no longer needed her: "When she saw her son was married and could be looked after, she proceeded to die" (qtd. in Woodall 232). Now that Borges was single again, the mother and son could make an attempt to return to their daily routines. Even in her nineties, Leonor continued to read aloud to her blind son.

However, Borges's duties as an internationally famous writer called him away from his mother's side. In 1971 he went on an eight-week trip that encompassed the United States, Europe, and the Middle East. All expenses were paid for, and di Giovanni and his wife accompanied Borges. Most of the trip was successful and enjoyable. Borges enjoyed Israel where he received the Jerusalem Prize, as well as the time he spent in London and Scotland. He especially delighted in a surprise trip that di Giovanni had arranged to Iceland. Studying Anglo-Saxon had led to Old Norse, and Borges was fascinated by the language and the Icelandic sagas. Borges, still very much interested in the languages, always looked for opportunities to feed his intellect. While he was at Oxford to receive an honorary degree, he even arranged to meet with a professor for a lesson in Anglo-Saxon.

Everywhere he went on the tour, Borges was praised and celebrated—except for a couple of political skirmishes along the way. On the first leg of the tour, Borges lectured at Columbia University in New York City, where he also received an honorary degree. The university sponsored a gathering of Latin American writers, intellectuals, and politicians, and over the course of the evening, one of the other writers criticized Borges for his refusal to engage in Latin America politics. Then, in the back of the room, a group of angry Puerto Rican students began protesting the university's racism. At some point in the midst of the uproar, one of the students yelled at Borges, "*hijo de puta*," accusing his mother of being a whore. Borges exploded, hitting his cane on the table, and challenging the young man to a duel.

He was also criticized while he was in London; an article in the *Guardian* condemned his politics. Woodall points out that although the article in some ways was on target, it also contained many simplistic generalizations. For example, the article claimed that "students, intellectuals, and revolutionaries no longer read [Borges];" Woodall counters that actually, "Argentine students, let alone revolutionaries, had hardly ever read Borges at all, though they knew exactly what he stood for: great writing, reactionary politics. Those Argentines and other Latin Americans who had actually read him tolerated the true naivete of his politics, while managing not to lose sight of his importance as a writer in Spanish" (Woodall 238). For the last twenty years of his life, Borges would often be criticized for what others considered old-fashioned, rigid views that remained stagnant in an ever-changing, complicated world.

During interviews, Borges provided political opinions if prompted, but he much preferred to discuss literature and language apart from politics. Borges, an extraordinary conversationalist, granted many interviews in his lifetime, and each one combined direct answers and evasive irony. He preferred meeting with people one-on-one, rather than in large groups. He charmed interviewers with his wit, and yet frustrated them by dodging questions. Rita Guibert observed that while he could be warm and friendly, he also exhibited anxiety, and "an extreme childlike impatience" (Burgin 42). In physical descriptions of Borges, interviewers often pointed out his failing eyes—the droop of one eyelid, and the curious combination of seeming both piercing and unfocused. He impressed people with his combination of frailty and vigor. The following description appears in a 1966 interview: "His walk is tentative, and he carries a cane, which he uses like a divining rod. He is short, with hair that looks slightly unreal in the way it rises from his head. His features are vague, softened by age, partially erased by the paleness of his skin" (Christ 113). Interviewers also often pointed out his big smile, and the way he grew more animated as he talked about literature.

Although Borges had granted a quick look into his personal life with "Autobiographical Essay," for the most part, he continued to foster the idea of his alter ego, "Borges," and the elusiveness of identity. During interviews he usually spent the time referencing other authors, and quoting his favorite works of literature. His incredible memory allowed him to store thousands of lines of verse, in Spanish, English,

French, German, or Latin, and he liked to recite these without prompting. His answers moved from seriousness to playful jabs, as he embraced both modesty and irony: "[My] work is a mere shavings," he told one interviewer. "I am just an international superstition, which is something, but I don't exist. I'm just a pretext, a prop. A mere prop" (Burgin 236). Borges was an amalgam of descriptions: a serious bibliophile who was often youthful and playful; a loquacious charmer, who could also be quite shy. An interviewer in 1966 captured Borges's personality:

> But when he laughs—and he laughs often—his features wrinkle into what actually resembles a wry question mark; and he is apt to make a sweeping or clearing gesture with his arm and to bring his hand down on the table. Most of his statements take the form of rhetorical questions, but in asking a genuine question, Borges displays now a looming curiosity, now a shy, almost pathetic incredulity. When he chooses, as in telling a joke, he adopts a crisp, dramatic tone, and his quotation from Oscar Wilde would do justice to an Edwardian actor. (Christ 113)

During the interviews, Borges often steered the questions away from his own work to discuss the work of his favorite authors. Just as Borges's political views rarely changed, neither did his literary tastes. As a self-educated intellectual, Borges ignored the canon and read what interested him, and the result was a highly esoteric list, heavy with secondary philosophers and obscure subjects, with gaps in the way of the classics. He also always remained faithful to the authors he had discovered in childhood and adolescence, often discussing Twain, Poe, or Kipling.

One might assume Borges, such a worldly intellectual, would foster highly sophisticated tastes, but he often surprised people. For example, Borges preferred musicals, such as *My Fair Lady*, to art-house films, and he never cultivated a taste for haute-cuisine food, preferring steak and *tortilla*. He never used drugs and rarely drank. He did not care for music, nor did he appreciate art; he was often blissfully unaware of contemporary artists and writers. In many respects, Borges lived in an ivory-tower of literature and language, and yet the same time, he was quite approachable and down to earth. Borges proved to be too complex and elusive in his political views and in his personality to categorize one way.

After the European tour, Borges returned to Buenos Aires, exhausted from traveling. He was also tired of the translations. He no longer wanted to return to the work, which he found too draining. The meetings with di Giovanni soon ended. In 1972 di Giovanni left Buenos Aires and went to live with his wife in England. Borges spent more of his time with another collaborator, a young woman who would stay with him until his death.

Last Years

María Kodama, of half-Argentine and half-Japanese descent, first met Borges in 1958, when she was twelve-years old. Her father had taken her to one of his lectures. Kodama was earning her doctorate in English at the University of Buenos Aries when she met Borges once again; in the late-sixties she joined his Anglo-Saxon and Old Norse study group. Kodama worked closely with Borges, even joining him and di Giovanni on the trip to Iceland. María spent significant time working as his secretary, and a close friendship began to develop.

Borges began to truly experience the benefits of being one of the most famous writers in the world—a fame that often puzzled him. Now that his marriage to Elsa was behind him and he no longer was required to work on the translations with di Giovanni, Borges felt freer than he ever had before. With this freedom came a desire to see the world. From 1972–85, Borges traveled extensively, and María was always with him. Borges's many travels offered a diversion and a way to enjoy his freedom, but they also served as a way to avoid the politically volatile climate of Argentina. Borges was adored and loved wherever he traveled, but at home, he was often criticized and even threatened for his unpopular views.

In 1973, one of Borges's worst nightmares came true: Perón was once again elected President. For many people of Argentina, who were tired of the violence and political turmoil, his return was a blessing. The sixties and seventies were a period of civil strife and revolving door of changing governments. However, Borges, as to be expected, was appalled. He resigned from his post at the National Library when Perón took office, and he spoke out against his return. Borges said in *Newsweek* that he did not fear the new government: "They know that if they hurt me it would cause an international uproar" (qtd. in Woodall 245). Borges was almost obsessed in his criticism of Perón. He ignored any of the effective programs that occurred during Perón's first reign, such as social welfare or labor benefits, and even his biographer Monegal admitted that Borges's views on Perón sometimes bordered on hysteria. Monegal explained that while he wanted to point out the finer, more complex points that Borges did not understand or overlooked, he realized his words would go unheard, asking, "how can one establish a dialogue with a dreamer?" (397). The Perón era was contradictory and complicated, and Borges's views on the matter were often limited and simplistic.

Many criticized Borges, including SADE, where he was once the president. SADE had reversed its anti-Perón position from the first reign and now supported Perón's return to power. Borges and his mother were even threatened by anonymous Perón supporters. Once Leonor answered the phone and the caller announced he was going to kill her. She gave him the address and told him to hurry up, as she was ninety-eight years old and would not last long (Woodall 246). Another time a bomb was placed outside of Borges's building. It did not go off, and the seventy-four-year-old Borges chastised the perpetrators: "Look how cowardly they are putting a bomb here. It would be easy enough to come up and attack me head-on. I always have my knife, don't I?" (qtd. in Woodall 246).

When Perón died in 1974, Borges did not shed any tears; however, Perón death was a disaster for most of the country. The following decade would become one of the most brutal periods in Argentina's modern history. Under his wife Isabel's leadership, guerrilla attacks and kidnappings began to become a way of life.

In his personal life, Borges encountered the loss of many friends as he grew older. He also experienced the death of his mother. Leonor was quite ill, and for the last two years, she clung onto life. It was an exhausting and consuming time for Borges. When she died in 1975, he was devastated, but her death also served as a release. Because of the prominent place she held in Borges's life, the ninety-nine-year-old Leonor was nearly as famous as her son, and there were many articles and obituaries. One published photograph of Borges weeping captured his devotion to his mother, and his profound grief in her death.

Despite his grief and the political turmoil, Borges continued to write. In July 1974, he had published *Obras completas*, which contained much of his poetry and all of his prose. The 1,200 page book was an instant success. He also published more books of poetry, as well as *El libro de arena* (*The Book of Sand*)—which appeared in print right before his mother's death. This was his last book of fiction, and at least in terms of commercial sale, it was his greatest success. This collection also contains his only love story, called "Ulrike."

Nobody knew the exact nature of Maria and Borges's relationship, except that Borges felt fortunate to have her company. "Having a woman half his age at his side when he might have otherwise been alone in this ambiance was one of the boons—perhaps the luckiest—of Borges' last years," states Woodall (243). Friends and biographers speculated that Borges and Maria probably did not have any sort of sexual relationship. They did not live together, and spent much of their time traveling and planning new trips. Most characterized the relationship as a combination of friendship, dependency, and compassion—and perhaps romance.

Although they now spent less time together, Borges continued to foster his friendship with Bioy, one of his last remaining friends. They dined together, and continued to collaborate; the jokes must have been a relief from the hostile political climate of Argentina. The two published their last detective collaboration in 1977.

For such a supposedly apolitical writer, Borges knew how to ignite quite a fury with his statements. He was once again making people angry. In March 1976, after Isabel was topped by the military, Borges welcomed the new leader, General Videla. Videla would oversee one of the bloodiest periods of violence in Argentina. The terrifying period of the *desaparecidos* (the disappeared) had begun; the military-ruled government arrested, kidnapped, and murdered an average of fifty left-wingers a week. When Borges lunched with Videla, the Left was appalled. Borges also made the grave mistake of visiting General Augusto Pinochet in Chile. These events, combined with racist remarks Borges made about the native people of his country, spurred angry criticism and threatened to tarnish his reputation as a great writer. His praise of the two dictators Videla and Pinochet alienated and discouraged many of his fans. One of the major results was that Borges was never awarded the Nobel Prize.

Ironically, Borges did not even consider himself political. In many respects, he was out of touch with current events, admitting, "I've never read newspapers.... I'm more interested in what occurred a long time ago than in current events" (Burgin 113). When he was pressed on his decision to meet with Pinochet, he tried to downplay the incident, explaining that he was in Chile for an award, and when the president invited him to dinner, he did not want to be rude, "I couldn't refuse, could I?" (Burgin 224). Borges was always a conservative; he even dedicated his translation of Walt Whitman's *Leaves of Grass* to President Nixon. Unlike many artists and writers, he never endorsed socialism or communism, and certainly feared the latter, which in part influenced his support for Videla. Despite his rigid views, Borges also continued to claim that he hoped one day for anarchy—"of having no government, having no police force, of being a kind people different from what we are now"—but believed now was not the right time and "government is a necessary evil" (Burgin 224). However, the threat of real anarchy, and the power of the masses, also frightened Borges; he did not trust the decisions of the people.

Despite his controversial viewpoints, many intellectuals continued to revere his work and ignore his politics, writing off his views as misunderstood and old-fashioned. Even the esteemed Pablo Neruda, a dedicated Marxist and one of the first victims of General Pinochet's dictatorship, expressed admiration for Borges's work:

> He's a great writer, and good heavens! All Spanish-speaking peoples are very proud that Borges exists.... But to quarrel with Borges, just because everyone wants to make me quarrel with Borges—that I'll never do. If he thinks like a dinosaur, that has nothing to do with my thinking. He doesn't understand a thing about what's happening in the modern world, and he thinks I don't either. Therefore, we are in agreement. (qtd. in Bell-Villada 43)

Eventually, Borges realized the Videla regime was corrupt and brutal, and he signed an open letter of protest about the disappeared. The military's campaign to wipe out what they considered left-wing terrorism was terrifying and appalling. Between 1976 and 1983, thousands of people, most of them dissidents and innocent civilians, were arrested and then vanished without a trace. Borges told the daily *La Prensa*: "I cannot ignore the serious moral problem created in the country by terrorism and repression. I cannot remain silent in the face of so many deaths, so many disappearances." He also spoke out against the Falklands War. However, despite his change of heart, many would never forget his early support for Videla.

Borges was realizing how chaotic politics were, and he truly did not want to concern himself with such issues. He was in the last years of his life, and he wanted to spend them freely with María. Now nearly completely blind, admitting that "the world has been becoming more and more blurred for me; books have lost their letters, my friends have lost their faces," Borges relied on María's young eyes to take him to new places (Burgin 33). He was no longer writing; instead of traveling to imaginary worlds, he wanted to physically travel to the real places. In these last thirteen years of travel, he visited Egypt, Japan, Morocco, Puerto Rico, Ecuador, the United States and Spain (11 times each), Paris, Geneva, Germany, and Britain. In 1984, Borges and María published a record of their travels called *Atlas*, in which Borges provided the text and María the photographs. The pictures, such as Borges touching a tiger for the first time or riding in a hot air balloon, depict his youthful enthusiasm and happiness.

Rarely ill throughout his life, Borges underwent prostate surgery in 1978; three years later, on his 81st birthday, he said, " I need to live, at least, one year more" (qtd. in Woodall 256). This was the year of his last published story, called "La memoria de Shakespeare" ("Shakespeare's Memory"). Borges received many more international awards, including awards from Spain and France.

Borges made his last stand in regards to his troubled home country by refusing to die in Argentina. Diagnosed with cancer of the liver, Borges went to Italy in 1985 and spent the winter there, before moving to Geneva—the place where he had chosen to die. Borges had always felt connected to Geneva: "For Borges it was natural to want to die in a place which, in his memory—perhaps the most compelling criterion for a man whose entire life had been lived through memory—was as much home to him as Buenos Aires" (Woodall 257). He felt safe in Geneva, away from the prying eyes of the media.

On April 24, 1986, Borges married María, a woman he had known for about twenty years and his constant companion for the final years of his life. Borges was eighty-seven years old; María was forty. The gossip reached Argentina—divorce still did not exist in Argentina law, and technically, Borges was still married to Elsa. Eventually, after a complicated process, the marriage was made legal—much to the dismay of many in Argentina, including Borges's sister and nephews (after his death, they launched a campaign against María in the local and European papers).

Eight weeks after the marriage, leaving behind one of the great literary legacies of the 20th century, Jorge Luis Borges died on June 14, 1986 and was buried in Geneva. María was named the sole inheritor of his estate, controlling all of Borges's copyright.

At times Borges was criticized for turning his back on Argentina. While many of his statements about politics could be troubling, Borges always identified as an Argentine writer. He may have occasionally turned his gaze to Europe, but he always considered Argentina his home. He romanticized the old Argentina, and often wrote about his country and his own complicated feelings about its setting, culture, and inhabitants. Many Latin American, as well as American, writers cite Borges as an important and monumental influence, and his spirit lives on through his many poems, fragments, and *ficciones*. In addition, he is memorialized at the Jorge Luis Borges Foundation house in Buenos Aires, established by Kodama, and in countless biographies and works of scholarship.

Works Cited

Bell-Villada, Gene H. *Borges and His Fiction: A Guide to His Mind and Art*. Revised Edition. Austin: University of Texas Press, 1999.

Borges, Jorge Luis. "Borges and I." *Labyrinths: Selected Stories & Other Writings*. Donald A. Yates and James Irby, eds. New York: A New Directions Book, 1962.

———. "Autobiographical Essay." *The Aleph and Other Stories, 1933–1969*. trans. Norman Thomas di Giovanni in collaboration with the author. New York, E. P. Dutton, 1970.

Burgin, Richard, ed. *Jorge Luis Borges: Conversations*. Jackson: University Press of Mississippi, 1998.

Christ, Ronald. "Interview." *Writers at Work: The Paris Review Interviews*. George Plimpton, ed. New York: The Viking Press, 1976. 109–146.

Rodriguez Monegal, Emir. *Jorge Luis Borges: A Literary Biography*. New York: Dutton, 1978.

Woodall, James. *Borges: A Life*. New York: Basic Books, 1996.

ELIZABETH BEAUDIN

Writing against Time

We have been graced over the centuries by a rich collection of storytellers: Mark Twain, Charles Dickens, Miguel de Cervantes, William Shakespeare, Dante, and Homer sit in the circular rows of Paradise accompanied by others who, defying generic boundaries, were a delight and benefit to their listeners and readers. Jorge Luis Borges belongs to the same pantheon. Like Twain, Borges offers crisp descriptions of eccentric and seemingly normal characters. Like Dickens, Borges drills down to the finest detail. Along with Cervantes, Borges plays with tradition and makes his own. In a fashion worthy of Shakespeare, Borges hones and expands language, taking possession of words in the process (In Spanish, who else owns the word "vertiginoso"?)[1] With Dante, Borges creates circles of light and darkness in his libraries of unseen and repetitive books. We do not ask if there was more than one Borges or whether his existence was merely legend; yet his blindness and ubiquity suggest striking similarities to a flesh and blood Homer.

    A storyteller who might also take a place in this group is one who told her own story as she wove the threads of 1001 others. Scheherazade carried her library of stories with her and recited them to a king; Borges imagined his tales—pulling details, characters, and events from his vast mental library—and later recited them to his many secretaries who took dictation for him over the years. Borges frequently cites the tales of a *Thousand and One Nights* in his works. Yet Scheherazade and Borges share a more fundamental link in their storytelling: a refutation of time.

In the case of Scheherazade, the more stories told, the more nights and mornings she fought off prescribed death. Though Borges faced no such mortal threat, the philosophy manifest in his written corpus—stories, poems, and essays—reveals a stubborn denial of time. Whether obviously analyzing time against the theories of other philosophers or playing with endless repetitions of images, objects, and intercalated plots, Borges leads his reader back and forth through his imaginings of a timeless state of being, bringing the reader to a point of skepticism that Borges considered fundamental to any act of reading.

From the beginning, Borges examines time and studies its philosophical permutations in his essays. In the title piece of *A History of Eternity* (*Historia de la eternidad*, 1936), Borges states openly his preoccupation: "For us, time is a jarring, urgent problem, perhaps the most vital problem of metaphysics, while eternity is a game or a spent hope." (*A* 123) Another essay entitled "The Duration of Hell" ("La duración del infierno," *Síntesis*, 1929 / *Discusión* 1932) looks at time for a different motive and speculated that contemplating the attribute of eternity truly produced horror. In these and other essays, Borges cites writers and philosophers that regularly inform his examinations of time; among these are Augustine, Berkeley, Dante, Hume, and Schopenhauer. As a result, he sets down a model of citations for his examinations of time and its philosophical permutations, such that we who cite Borges continue his cycle of eternal return.[2]

In 1940, Borges quotes for his readers in "The Mirror of Enigmas" ("El espejo de los enigmas," *Sur* 1940 / *Otras inquisiciones* 1952, 1960) a citation of León Bloy: "No man knows who he is." (*L* 212) Borges thus posits a fundamental question regarding existence, not necessarily related to identity as would be expected but to a paradigm of time since existence and identity are inextricably linked with time. In "Circular Time," written in 1941 and added to the collection *History of Eternity* in 1961, Borges expands the model to include and/or juxtapose classical theories held by many regularly studied and cited by Borges.[3] Here, a collection, traversing many years, including Plato, Marcus Aurelius, and Bertand Russell offers Borges a backdrop from which he can agree or reject or extrapolate. Years later in "Pascal's Sphere," ("La esfera de Pascal", *La Nación*, 1951; *Otras inquisiciones* 1952, 1960) his model of citation looks at Renaissance figures within the context of metaphors to understand the strength of thought produced when contemplating a sphere.[4] In this case, Borges shifts from his temporal debate to a spatial one but applies the Renaissance understanding of systems of astrology and the existence of space only to loop back onto yet another reflection of time.

Two other essays composed in the intervening years are fundamental to Borges as the philosopher and the storyteller concerned and obsessed with time. In 1948, Borges published a small pamphlet called "The New Refutation of Time" (Buenos Aires., *Oportet y Haereses*, 1947 / *Otras Inquisiciones*, 1952, 1960). The citation model seen in this and other essays sets out Borges's basic and quite startling message: *I deny time*. In 1949, he writes a lovely short essay entitled "The Partial Magic of the *Quixote*" ("Magias parciales del Quijote," *La Nación*, 1949 / *Otras Inquisiciones*, 1952, 1960) in which his citation model effectively links Borges's denial of time with his appreciation of Cervantes's craft of storytelling.

Daunting as the essays of Borges may seem, the reader can begin to probe Borges's published works by seeking out this same theory of time in some of his stories and most recognized poems. The many voices compiled in what we know today as the *Thousand and One Nights* are related by one voice that brings together in Scheherazade's stories an endless list of mythical, popular and religious sources. Borges, in turn, proceeds from a compilation of ideas, the product of his voracious studying, such that it may appear that a short story or essay requires of the reader an equally vast preparation to keep up. Yet, if in the essays Borges desires to postulate his metaphysics, perhaps in his stories he merely wishes that his reader succumb to a healthy skepticism by accepting his catalog of ideas, citations, and images—the equivalent of Scheherazade's library of tales. Like King Shariar listening each night to Scheherazade's endless tales, the reader of Borges eventually learns to sit back, listen or, in this case, read and give herself over to the master.

When first approaching the essay "The Partial Magic of the *Quixote*," for example, what does the reader make of the title of this short essay? The English translation is faithful to the original title: "Magias parciales del 'Quijote'" (*Otras inquisiciones* 1952, 1960). The word that catches the reader at first glance is *partial*. Does Borges suggest here from the outset that Cervantes's work is only partially magical? His opening line taunts as well. For Borges it does not matter whether his observations may have appeared before, what matters to him is their possible penetration of the truth. Then Borges, in a somewhat offhanded manner, aligns Cervantes's work with other great classical texts, yet labels the *Quixote* as a realistic work as if to suggest some inferiority in passing. Immediately though, Borges shifts the comparison to the realism of the 19th century, mentioning Joseph Conrad and Henry James as examples, to posit that Cervantes both exceeded the classical limits and conquered the 19th century restrictions to produce a truly original work in which Cervantes was able "to counterpose a real prosaic world to an imaginary poetic world." (*L* 193)

What matters here is not the observation, much like Borges's dismissal of repeated observations at the opening of the essay, but rather how Borges comes to his conclusion and what ramification the conclusion has for the reading of his short fiction. The essay tests any reader's cultural and intellectual preparation by citing not only James and Conrad, but many others such as Spanish poets (Unamuno, Azorín, and Machado), Carlyle, Moses of León, as well as a poem by Valmiki.

The essential argument rests, though, in two texts: the *Quixote* and the *Thousand and One Nights*. And for his argument, Borges provides details; a technique he couples with citing earlier or contemporary authorities, as if Borges wants to take the reader by the hand. He explains that in chapter six of Part I of the *Quixote*, the priest and the barber examine the books in Don Quixote's library. Along with the many novels of chivalry and pastoral novels, the two come across the *Galatea*, written by Cervantes in 1585. The barber confesses to being a friend of the *Galatea*'s author. In chapter nine of the *Quixote*, the reader learns that Cervantes created the *Quixote* from a manuscript acquired in Toledo and later translated from the original Arabic by a *morisco* he hired. Then, in Part II, one discovers that the barber and the priest have read the first part, thus protagonists of both parts of the novel are also readers of the text in which they appear.

In the case of the *Thousand and One Nights*, we know that King Shariar having been betrayed by his first wife now follows the policy of marrying a virgin bride only to kill her the morning after the honeymoon. Scheherazade, determined to break this painful tradition and thus save herself from this fate, sets out to tell the King a new story each night. Borges notes that on night 602, King Shariar hears his own story. Borges contends that this intercalation of tales goes far beyond the framed retelling in Shakespeare's *Hamlet* of a king's death when Hamlet has actors reenact the murder of his father. Borges believes that by Scheherazade retelling the same story that opened the *Thousand and One Nights* the full compendium of tales becomes circular and thus infinite. The title, used by Sir Richard Burton in Borges's preferred translation, points to the infinite. In the lecture given in Buenos Aires in 1977 on the *Thousand and One Nights*, Borges compares the title to the English expression 'forever and a day.' Borges speculates further:

> Why were there first a thousand and later a thousand and one? I think there are two reasons. First, there was the superstition—and superstition is very important in this case—that even numbers are evil omens. They then sought an odd number and luckily added *and one*. If they had made it nine hundred and ninety-nine we would have felt that there was a night missing. This way we feel that we have been given something infinite, that we have received a bonus, another night.[5]

What Borges suggests here regarding the title of the *Thousand and One Nights* is similar to what the Beatles captured in their song "Eight Days a Week." Unlike today's wearisome expression "24/7," the line that says, "I will love you eight days a week" conjures up a similar sense of the infinite.

Like King Shariar, the readers of Part II of the *Quixote* are themselves protagonists. What Borges identifies as disturbing in both cases is simple: "these inversions suggest that if the characters of a fictional work can be readers or spectators, we, its readers or spectators, can be fictitious." (*L* 196) Thus, the statement "No man knows who he is" as stated by León Bloy and repeated by Jorge Luis Borges begins to take on unexpected dimensions.

Perhaps the best fictional manifestation of Borges's argument in "The Partial Magic of the *Quixote*" is his story entitled "The Circular Ruins" ("Las ruinas circulares," *Sur* 1940 / *Ficciones* 1956). Its epithet—here a citation of eminent popular value to an English-speaking audience—essentially warns the reader straightaway. It is a quote from Lewis Carroll's *Through the Looking-Glass* and speaks of dreaming. Borges is about to take the reader down the rabbit hole.

The story tells of an unnamed protagonist who appears unexpectedly in a "swampy wilderness" (*A* 55). There are few defining markers in the area with which the reader might attach any realistic labels, except the man, the circular temple in ruins that he finds, and a stone image, unrecognizable because of the destruction of time. What the reader notices is that the man spends more time asleep than awake, and for a startling reason: "His guiding purpose, though it was supernatural, was not impossible. He wanted to dream a man; he wanted to dream him down to the last detail and project him into the world of reality." (*A* 56) Not to dream of a man, but to dream one up.

His initial dreams are chaotic and drain his strength. For several nights, he dreams of teaching a classroom full of pupils and focuses his attention on one in particular. Resentfully, the dreamer abandons this first attempt and decides to start fresh after rebuilding his strength. When the moon is full again, he bathes in the river's water and completes ritual prayers invoking the name of an all-powerful god. Immediately he falls asleep and dreams of a heart: "... throbbing, warm, secret. It was the size of a closed fist, a darkish red in the dimness of a human body still without a face or sex." (*A* 58) With great patience, the dreamer concentrates on the heart for the next two weeks of dreams. On day fourteen, he permits himself the luxury of touching the heart in his dream and is satisfied. Over the next year, the dreamer proceeds thoughtfully until the young man that has taken form in his dreams is now whole but still unable to stand or speak.

During the process, the dreamer prays regularly to the gods. On one frustrating occasion, the man prays to the stone idol. Prostrating himself before the image, the man falls asleep and dreams that the idol speaks to him. The stone figure identifies itself as the god Fire and reveals to the man that the world will see his dreamt creation as a man and that only Fire and the man will know the truth. Fire ordains that the man instruct his creation in the appropriate rituals and send him on to the ruined temple down river. It is then that the dreamed creation awakes in the man's dream. The dreamer follows Fire's instructions carefully. He lovingly teaches his dreamed creation as he would a son and finally sends him off to the other temple.

Once done with his task, the man sleeps as others do, without dreams of creation. After a long period of time, two men from the river wake the dreamer and tell him of a magic man who can walk on fire without being burned. The dreamer's initial joy is quickly replaced by fear for his dreamt son. He worries that his creation will somehow discover that he is a mere illusion in the minds of men. At the same time, the dreamer witnesses a drastic change in his surroundings. The animals' behavior foretells the approach of a devastating fire. The dreamer considers saving himself in the river but realizes that what awaits him will end his many years of labor. As the fire nears, the dreamer walks into its flames. "They did not bite into his flesh, but caressed him and flooded him without heat or burning. In relief, in humiliation, in terror, he understood that he, too, was an appearance, that someone else was dreaming him." (*A* 62)

Unlike his essays and many of his short stories, this tale of Borges is not overwhelming in its citations, despite passing references to the Greek language and the Gnostics. But the Lewis Carroll epithet is telling and the lack of references is equally compelling. Borges takes the reader into the dreams of the dreamer at face value. And in the end leaves the reader with a problem similar to that faced in the *Quixote* and the *Thousand and One Nights*. Here, Borges's denial of time is not framed by his metaphysics or the philosophy of others; rather, Borges speaks directly to the imagination of the reader.

In "The Art of Poetry" ("*Arte poética,*" *Límites* 1958 / *Antología poética* 1961), Borges provides a similar opportunity for his readers to dream a circular time.

> To gaze at a river made of time and water
> and remember Time is another river
> To know we stray like a river
> and our faces vanish like water.
>
> To feel that waking is another dream
> that dreams of not dreaming and that the death
> We fear in our bones is the death
> that every night we call a dream.
>
> To see in every day and year a symbol
> of all the days of man and his years,
> and convert the outrage of the years
> into a music, a sound and a symbol.

> To see in death a dream, in the sunset
> a golden sadness—such is poetry,
> humble and immortal, poetry
> returning, like dawn and sunset.
>
> Sometimes at evening there's a face
> that sees us from the deeps of a mirror.
> Art must be that sort of mirror,
> disclosing to each of us his face.
>
> They say Ulysses, wearied of wonders
> wept with love on seeing Ithaca,
> humble and green. Art is that Ithaca,
> a green eternity, now wonders.
>
> Art is endless like a river flowing,
> passing, yet remaining, a mirror to the same
> inconstant Heraclitus, who is the same
> and yet another, like the river flowing.
>   Trans. Anthony Kerrigan
>   (*PA* 199; compare *S–P* 137)

Here, Borges sheds the arrogance of citing myriad philosophers and his own pose of denying time. Yet, his denial still controls his definitions of Art and Poetry. Citing "inconstant Heraclitus" reminds the reader that one cannot step into the same river twice. The circular process of dreaming a creation and seeing it walk through flames described in "The Circular Ruins" becomes much like the endless river of Poetry defined here. The poet, bound by an everlasting anxiety of influence, writes anew what has been written and will be written again, the same and yet not.

Both the poem and the short story loop back onto thoughts Borges postulated earlier in his essay "Circular Time" in which he recalls the worlds of Heraclitus and Seneca as being engendered by fire and renewed by water. In the same essay, Borges negates two concepts: the reality of a past and a future, and all novelty. Like the dreamer, Borges engenders a perfect circle of happenings—to avoid here the word *time*—and as a poet he battles the restriction imposed on him by language, which requires writing in a linear fashion, thus implying a beginning and an end. In his poem, the mirrors, the outrage, the humble wonders of returning converge in the river that both remains and flows on. Dreams and poetry break the restraints and permit Borges his denial of time.

In the essay "Pascal's Sphere," circularity is all encompassing. The opening and closing sentences of the essay—notoriously Borgesian in their similarity and difference—frame a recitation of quick references from a series of intellectuals. Among them is Giordano Bruno, who associated the circle with divinity. Bruno's premise that "the universe is all center, or that the center of the universe is everywhere and the circumference nowhere" (*L* 191) is similar to that of Pascal, who wrote more than a century later: "Nature is an infinite sphere, the center of which is everywhere, the circumference nowhere." (*L* 192) Borges believes though that, unlike Bruno whose musings on the circle represented metaphysical liberation, Pascal was plagued by the weight of the natural world, suggesting that by seeing nature as a frightful sphere he becomes much like a poet trying to escape the confines of language. Such that Borges concludes: "It may be that universal history is the history of the different intonation given a handful of metaphors." (*L* 192; *CN–F* 353)

This handful of metaphors could indeed characterize the refracted permutations of ideas, surroundings, and images that Borges's short stories exhibit. One of the most recognizable stories is "The Aleph" ("El Aleph," *Sur* 1945; *Ficciones* 1956). The title is taken from the first letter of the Hebrew alphabet. The story describes the uncanny existence of a spherical spot in the cellar of a Buenos Aires house that is home to the eccentric Carlos Argentino Daneri. In the little sphere found on the nineteenth step of the cellar stairs, one sees the entire universe. A less known story entitled "The Zahir" ("El Zahir," *Anales de Buenos Aires*, 1947; *El Aleph* 1952) offers the metaphorical inverse of "The Aleph." The title comes from an Arabic word, an attribute of Allah (*Qur'an* LVII: 3), meaning visible or evident.

Borges states at the beginning of his story that the Zahir is a common 20 centavo coin used in Buenos Aires. Parenthetically though, he explains that it is and has been everything: a tiger, an astrolabe, a blind man, a compass, as well as "a vein running through the marble in one of the twelve hundred columns" in the mosque at Córdoba. (*PA* 128; *L* 156; *C–F* 242) Not surprisingly, as in "The Aleph," Borges is both protagonist and author and comes into possession of the Zahir on the day after a funeral; this time for Teodelina Villar, a woman more interested in perfection than in beauty. "She sought the Absolute ... but the Absolute in the momentary. Her life was exemplary, and yet an inner despair unremittingly gnawed her. She attempted continual metamorphoses ..." (*PA* 129; *L* 157; *C–F* 243) When her family fell into economic difficulties, Teodelina abandoned her quest for perfection as she realized "... that the exercise of her art required a fortune. She chose to retire rather than to bungle." (*PA* 129; *L* 157; *C–F* 243)

The person of Teodelina combines elements of both Carlos Argentino, the obsessed composer of a poem describing all known things and owner of the Aleph, and Beatriz Viterbo, Carlos's cousin and object of Borges's unrequited love. In "The Aleph", Borges develops a peculiar relationship with Daneri after Beatriz' death. In "The Zahir", Borges the protagonist confesses to being enamored of Teodelina and he becomes plagued by the coin given him at a bar after he leaves Teodelina laid out in her coffin, at once rigid and perfect.

Is he feverish or drunk? Borges the protagonist is not sure. He is obsessed by the universality of the coin; it conjures up images of Ahab's gold piece, Leopold Bloom's florin, Judas's thirty pieces, and so many others. The day after receiving the coin, Borges wrestles with ways of losing it in order to "get out of its orbit." (*PA* 132; *L* 159; *C–F* 245) Randomly selecting a bar on one of his walks, the protagonist pays for his drink with the Zahir. He returns home to occupy himself by writing a new story. The deliberate loss of the coin and the diversion of writing have limited effect. A month later Borges, after visiting a psychiatrist, unexpectedly finds a book documenting the Zahir in splendid detail. Yet repeated readings of the book only serve to increase his despair. Here, like the letter and the compass described in the 1947 postscript to "Tlön, Uqbar, Orbis Tertius" (*Sur* 1940 / *Ficciones* 1956), documents and ephemera notoriously appear out of nowhere to attach plausibility to otherwise apocryphal or disappearing data.

Borges ends "The Zahir" explaining that his fate shall be eternally linked to the coin: "I shall pass from thousands of apparitions to one alone: from a very complex dream to a very simple dream. Others will dream that I am mad, and I shall dream of the Zahir. And when everyone on earth thinks of the Zahir day and night, which will be a dream and which a reality, the earth or the Zahir?" (*PA* 137; *L* 164; *C–F* 248–249)

This coin, representing all coins and eventually all things, is quite visible to Borges from the outset. The Aleph, however, is an unseen treasure owned by Daneri. Borges first sees the "small iridescent sphere" in the full darkness of Daneri's basement. Mocking the format of many essays and repeating a technique used in other tales, Borges ends "The Aleph" with a postscript dated March, 1943. In it Borges quotes Sir Richard Burton, his preferred translator of the *Thousand and One Nights*, who documented some of the many meanings for the word Aleph. One of these curiously states: "The Faithful who attend the Mosque of Amr, in Cairo, know very well that the universe is in the interior of one of the stone columns surrounding the central courtyard ... No one, of course, can see it ..." (*PA* 154; *A* 30; *C–F* 285) Do the convergences of these stories suggest that Borges has run out of original material? Has he caught himself in an Eternal Return of his own making? Or, as the reader over time comes to learn, is Borges once again encouraging both submission and simultaneous skepticism on the part of his readers?

A similar tension between the visible and the invisible is at the heart of the pivotal and celebrated story called "Pierre Menard, Author of Don Quixote." ("Pierre Menard, autor del Quijote," *Sur* 1939 / *Ficciones* 1956) The tale came at a critical juncture for Borges. He was recovering from septicemia, the result of a fluke accident in which he scraped his forehead against a casement window. This event later figures in a story of his entitled "The South" ("El Sur," *La Nación* 1953 / *Ficciones* 1956). During his recovery, Borges doubted his ability ever to write again because of the fevers and hallucinations he battled. He challenged himself to write a story; the reception of which would determine for Borges whether or not he should continue to write.[6]

What resulted from this challenge is now legendary. Borges begins the oft-quoted tale of the eccentric Pierre Menard by listing his visible bibliography. The opening format of the story mimics many of Borges's earlier essays.[7] The citations and footnotes, heavy with dates and details, give the appearance of non-fictional facts as Borges describes the minutia that represents the published work of friend Menard. But it is the "subterranean" opus of the late Pierre Menard that Borges, the first person narrator of the tale, feels compelled to reveal: "This work, perhaps the most significant of our time, consists of the ninth and thirty-eighth chapters of the first part of *Don Quixote* and a fragment of chapter twenty-two.... He did not want to compose another *Quixote*—which is easy—but *the Quixote itself.*" (*L* 38–39; *C–F* 90)

Borges proceeds to rationalize the absurdity of Menard's project. The style Borges chooses further parodies his earlier essays and critical writing style in general. This tactic is much like that used "The Approach to Al-Mu'tasim" ("El acercamiento a Almotásim," *Historia de la eternidad*, 1936 / *Ficciones* 1956), the fictional tale that lampooned critical book reviews that Borges mischievously published with a collection of essays. Playing with a non-fictional style further exaggerates the impossible intentions of Menard in that he must "know Spanish well, recover the Catholic faith, fight against the Moors or the Turk, forget the history of Europe between the years 1602 and 1918, *be* Miguel de Cervantes." (*L* 40; *C–F* 91)

Borges, the narrator, adjudges Menard's style as subtler than that of Cervantes. To compares the two texts, the narrator cites a passage from both, which by default is exactly alike:

> ... truth, whose mother is history, rival of time, depository of deeds, witness of the past, exemplar and adviser to the present, and the future's counselor. (*L* 43)

This is genius on the part of Menard, according to the narrator, because "Historical truth, for him, is not what has happened; it is what we judge to have happened." (*L* 43) Thus, Menard has honed in on the essential truth that time exists only as we perceive it; falsely, in other words. Borges goes even further in tweaking the nose of his audience, and his own for that matter, when he alleges that any exercise of the intellect, in philosophy or literature, ends up out of date and useless. So, when the narrator concludes his story of Menard, it is no surprise that he suggests reading "the *Odyssey* as if it were posterior to the *Aeneid*" (*L* 44) since friend Menard has flipped the universe on its back. There is no historical truth because Menard has written the *Quixote*. There is no time since Borges has written Menard writing Cervantes. Is he the dreamer or the one dreamed?

Borges answers his own question with regularity in his work and particularly in his prose poem (or 'parable' as it is called in the collection *Labyrinths*) "Borges and I" ("Borges y yo," *La Biblioteca* 1957 / *El hacedor* 1961) when he explains that he has tried to escape this doubling of self:

"... Years ago I tried to free myself from him, and I went from the mythologies of the city suburbs to games with time and infinity, but now those games belong to Borges, and I will have to think up something else. Thus is my life a flight, and I lose everything, and everything belongs to oblivion, or to him.

I don't know which one of the two of us is writing this page."

Trans. Anthony Kerrigan (*PA* 200–201; compare *L* 246–247; *S–P* 93)

So, unlike the specificity found in earlier poems, for example ("Recoleta Cemetery" or "A Page to Commemorate Colonel Suárez, Victor at Junín"), Borges toys with doubled identities. Plurality and sameness figure as well in "Poem of the Gifts" ("El poema de los dones," *Poemas* 1959 / *El hacedor* 1961):

> Wandering through the heavy galleries,
> I often feel with sacred vague horror
> That I am that other, the dead one, who will
> Have walked here too and on these very days.
>
> Which of us is writing this poem
> With plural I and a single darkness?
> What difference the word that names me
> If the curse is undivided and single?
>
> Groussac or Borges, I look at this dear
> World which collapses and goes out
> In a pale indefinite ash
> That resembles both the dream and oblivion.

Trans. Irving Feldman
(*PA* 195; compare *S–P* 95–97)

Here the final chapter of his gradual blindness inspires a comparison of the dualities he possesses. Written at the time he was appointed Director of the National Library, Borges documents the fact that uncannily he shared blindness with two previous directors, José Mármol and Paul

Groussac.[8] The "plural I" of this poem echoes the statement ending "Borges and I" within the context of facing the books he loves in total darkness.[9] The convergence of self parallels the meeting of times; his and that of his predecessors, for example. More compelling is the phrase "una pálida ceniza vaga" translated as "pale indefinite ash" which in one expression captures the remaining color left to Borges and the denial of time and death wrapped up in dreams and oblivion in the space most associated with Borges—the library.[10]

Perhaps it is Borges's desire for anachronicity that defines his "games with time and infinity" as well as his life. Despite Borges's extensive and enviable preparation in world history and letters, his political views were notoriously out of sync with the events taking place around him, both in his native Argentina and the world.[11] More importantly, Borges's defiance of time informs his entire corpus. Is it because of his mutiny with time that Borges so often compiled and recompiled collections of poems, stories, and essays to the frustration of academics and publishers alike? Where or which is the authoritative text?[12] The fact that there is no Ur-Borges has further frustrated the translations of Borges's works into other languages.[13] In the English translations alone, the same story appears in several collections translated by even more individuals producing textual permutations that are truly vertiginous, thus truly Borgesian.

If an authoritative glimpse into Borges exists, it might be found in "The New Refutation of Time." (*Nueva refutación del tiempo*, 1947 / *Otras inquisiciones* 1952, 1960) Curiously the essay's format is much like a framed narrative. The prologue introduces the two sections. A footnote closes the frame. The opening of the prologue—its conditional verb tense, in particular—at once places the essay in a temporal frame and then immediately withdraws it:

> Had this refutation (or even the title) been published in the middle of the eighteenth century, it would survive in Hume's bibliographies.... But published in 1947—post Bergson—it is an anachronistic *reductio ad absurdum* of a preterite system or, what is worse, the feeble artifice of an Argentinian gone astray in the maze of metaphysics. (*PA* 44; compare *L* 217; *CN–F* 317)

Does Borges here intend to add his own name to the philosophical canon by surviving in Hume's bibliographies? Is his ploy similar to Dante's naming himself among the circle of great poets in the first circle of Hell? It seems more likely that Borges's opening declaration accentuates the limitations of his words both temporally as well as metaphysically.

Curiously, like the details provided at the outset of "Pierre Menard, Author of the *Quixote*," Borges explains the genealogy of the essay. It is the joining of two previous versions, labeled A and B, the second being a revision of the first. He acknowledges that the title (a *new* refutation) would cause problems for logicians in his audience. And Borges then sets everyone up:

> ... for to say that a refutation of time is new (or old, for that matter) is to attribute to it a temporal predicate, thus restoring at once the very notion the subject strives to destroy. Still and all I shall let it stand, so that its ever-so-slight mockery gives proof that I do not overrate the importance of this play on words. And then, too, our language is so thoroughly saturated and animated with the notion of time that quite possibly not a single sentence in all these pages fails to require or invoke it. (PA 45; compare *L* 218, *CN–F* 317–318)

Borges takes the idea of *mise en texte* to new heights and prepares to refute time while recognizing the impossibility of such a task. The essay is really two and as the reader will discover, Section A Part II is yet another essay inserted for clarification ("Feeling in Death," originally published as "Sentirse en muerte," *El idioma de los argentinos* 1928).[14] Borges not only practices auto-citation but compiles citations from his working library of philosophers to present their views in order to argue against and to define or deny his own.

Sections A and B share similarities in format. Borges cites metaphysical theories; first those of Berkeley and Leibniz and then of Hume and Schopenhauer, among many others. In each section, Borges offers examples of a suspension of time characteristic of dreams and memories: first, a scene from Huckleberry Finn in section A; then in section B, the dream of Chuang Tzu. The Chinese man dreamt he was a butterfly, but on awaking was not sure if he was a man who dreamt of a butterfly or a butterfly who dreamt of a man. In Huck's case, stars, the river, and his dream converge. Borges uses Huck's example to go beyond the arguments of idealism to a series of assertions that he begins with "I deny" to refute the existence of succession and contemporaneity.

Yet beyond these overt declarations in Section A, its beginning is notably different from its partner B in that Borges lists previous works of his own in which he contends to have "glimpsed or foreseen" a refutation of time. In Section A Part II, Borges includes his earlier essay "Feeling in Death," saying that this intercalated note may help where the confines of successive language and time hinder. Like the examples provided in the main sections of A and B, the illustration here is an evening stroll of undetermined destination. The surroundings' familiarity provokes the realization that Borges had walked the same streets thirty years earlier. This leads to imagining himself in the same locale only in the 1800's. He concludes— simultaneously Section A and "Feeling in Death"—by maintaining:

> ... That pure representation of homogeneous objects—the night in serenity, a limpid little wall, the provincial scent of the honeysuckle, the elemental earth—is not merely identical to the one present on that corner so many years ago, it is, without resemblances or repetitions, the very same. Time ... is a delusion: the difference and inseparability of one moment belonging to its apparent past from another belonging to its apparent present is sufficient to disintegrate it. (*L* 226–227; *PA* 55; *CN–F* 325)

The phrase "without resemblances or repetitions" ("sin parecidos ni repeticiones") attempts to eliminate the ambiguity Borges has labored with in the essay precisely because of the succession of time implied in a linearly written language. There is no wiggle room here. Time may be a delusion but its contradiction is enough to cause its own disintegration.

The format that ends Section B follows the gist of Borge's uncompromising stance and takes it a step further. The revision written in 1946 ends on a gloomier and much more personal note:

> *And yet, and yet* ... Denying temporal succession, denying the self, denying the astronomical universe, are apparent

desperations and secret consolations.... Time is the substance I am made of. Time is a river which sweeps me along, but I am the river; it is a tiger which destroys me, but I am the tiger; it is a fire which consumes me, but I am the fire. The world, unfortunately, is real; I, unfortunately, am Borges. (*L* 233–234; *PA* 64, *CN–F* 332)

The "foreseen glimpse" and the "plural I" disintegrate along with time as Borges confesses he is stuck, like the writers he cites.

In his lecture on the *Thousand and One Nights*, one of seven nights of lectures, Borges delights in the fact that Galland, the first Western translator of Scheherazade's tales, had apparently added a story of his own to the translation, that of Aladdin and the magic lamp.[15] Even more amusing for Borges was that DeQuincey, years later, wrote in his autobiography that Aladdin's story is superior to the others, yet he described it differently than Galland had. Borges dismisses the fact that DeQuincey's comments could have resulted from an overactive imagination. He discards the aspersions against Galland for tampering with the text. Instead, Borges speaks, perhaps with "secret consolations," of the continuity of the text. In like fashion, Borges perseveres with his stories. Like Scheherazade and the stories in the *Thousand and One Nights*, Borges inserts and reasserts texts, citations, and images into his own. And like the philosopher Spinoza whose rational system of metaphysics he admired and often cited, Borges stubbornly seeks the infinite in a text he polishes over and over again.

"Spinoza"
("Spinoza," *Nueva antología poética* 1969 / *El otro, el mismo* 1969)
   Here in the twilight the translucent hands
   Of the Jew polishing the crystal glass.
   The dying afternoon is cold with bands
   Of fear. Each day the afternoons all pass
   The same. The hands and space of hyacinth
   Paling in the confines of the ghetto walls
   Barely exists for the quiet man who stalls
   There, dreaming up a brilliant labyrinth.
   Fame doesn't trouble him (that reflection of
   Dreams in the dream of another mirror), nor love,

The timid love women. Gone the bars,
He's free, from metaphor and myth, to sit
Polishing a stubborn lens: the infinite
Map of the One who now is all His stars.
    Trans. Willis Barnstone (*S–P* 229; compare *SP* 193)

Notes

1. For valuable insight regarding Borges's command of Spanish and how this relates to translations in English, see the conversation between Borges and Norman Thomas di Giovanni in *Borges on Writing*. Ed. Norman Thomas di Giovanni, et al. New York, E. P. Dutton, 1973. pp. 103–160.

2. This is Lisa Block de Behar's point of departure in *Borges: The Passion of an Endless Quotation* where she states: "... if Borges quotes innumerable authors in his works, it should not surprise us that innumerable authors continue to quote Borges. Recourse and recurrence, from one author to the other: literary passion manages to order itself around quotations that animate an inconclusive textual game." (p. 1)

3. The essay collected as "El tiempo circular" in the 1961 edition of *Historia de la eternidad* first appeared as "Tres formas del eterno regreso" in *La Nación* in 1941.

4. A valuable comparative essay from Borges on metaphors is of course "The Kennigars" ("Las kenningar" in *Historia de la eternidad*, 1936) in which Borges studies the Icelandic tropes popular until 100 AD.

5. Jorge Luis Borges. *Seven Nights*. Trans. Eliot Weinberger. New York: New Directions, 1984. pp. 45 and 49.

6. Borges recounts his accident and his brush with death in his "Autobiographical Essay," an original essay collected with English translations of previous short stories in *The Aleph and Other Stories*. Ed. and trans. Norman Thomas di Giovanni. New York: E. P. Dutton, 1970. pp. 242–243.

7. In fact, Borges thought the story was "a kind of essay." See his interview with Richard Burgin in *Jorge Luis Borges: Conversations*. Jackson: University of Mississippi Press, 1998. p. 15.

8. For Borges's recounting of his blindness and his appointment as Director of the National Library, see his "Autobiographical Essay" in *The Aleph and Other Stories*. Ed. and trans. Norman Thomas di Giovanni. New York: E. P. Dutton, 1970. pp. 249 ff. See his interview with Richard Burgin in *Jorge Luis Borges: Conversations*. Jackson: University of Mississippi Press, 1998. pp. 43–45.

9. See Silvia Molloy's splendid discussion of 'many-to-one' affirmations in Borges's work causing, as Professor Molloy states, a disarticulation or "fissure

that Borges never loses sight of" in the chapter "Pleasure and Perplexity" in *Signs of Borges*. Durham: Duke University Press, 1994. pp. 95–111.

10. For a rigorous examination of the library in Borges's work, see Lisa Block de Behar's chapter on "The Place of the Library" in her *The Passion of an Endless Quotation*. Trans. William Egginton. New York: State University of New York, 2003.

11. See the chapter "Borges Global" in James Woodall's very effective *The Man in the Mirror of the Book* for a thorough discussion of the many delicate political moments in Borges's career; for example, citing the Alamo in Mexico City, praising Ben Gurion after the 1967 Arab-Israeli War, and Borges's anti-Castro position. These facts in conjunction with the anti-Perón stance that Borges maintained may explain the questionable decision by the Nobel committee to sidestep Borges, but does not in any way justify the gaffe. See also Emir Rodríguez Monegal. *Jorge Luis Borges: A Literary Biography*. New York: Dutton, 1978.

12. The labyrinth of versions dealing with Borges's poems is truly too vertiginous to comment in a short space. His short fiction, however, can provide a quick glimpse at the trajectory of texts available. For example, the story "Pierre Menard, autor del *Quijote*" first appeared in *Sur*, no. 56 (1939). It was collected in *El jardín de los senderos que se bifurcan* in 1941 which then became Part One of *Ficciones*, published in 1944; the "canonical" Spanish edition of *Ficciones* is that published by Emecé in 1956 in Buenos Aires. Of the English translations of the story, compare: *Labyrinths: Selected Stories & Other Writings*. Ed. Donald Yales and James E. Irby. New York: New Directions, 1964; *Ficciones*, Ed. John Sturrock, New York: Knopf, 1993; and *Collected Fiction*. Trans. by Andrew Hurley. New York: Penguin, 1998.

13. In the conversation on translation with Borges, Norman Thomas di Giovanni recounts that "a professor complained about Borges's tampering with his work.... One of the great luxuries of working with Borges is that he's interested only in making things better and not in defending a text." *Borges on Writing*. Ed. Norman Thomas di Giovanni, et al. New York, E. P. Dutton, 1973. p. 158. See also James Woodall's lament for the state of Borges's body of work in Spanish as well as English in James Woodall. *The Man in the Mirror of the Book*. London: Hodder & Stoughton, 1996. p. 280.

14. This same note also appears inserted in the essay "History of Eternity" in the collection by the same name. (*Historia de la eternidad* 1936)

15. See Borges's lecture "The Thousand and One Nights" in *Seven Nights*, pp. 42–57.

Abbreviations of Works by Jorge Luis Borges Cited in the Text

A *The Aleph and Other Stories, 1933–1969*. Ed. and trans. by Norman Thomas di Giovanni in collaboration with the author. New York: E. P. Dutton, 1970.

C–F *Collected Fiction*. Trans. by Andrew Hurley. New York: Penguin, 1998.

CN–F *Selected Non-Fiction*. Ed. Eliot Weinberger. New York: Penguin, 1999.

L *Labyrinths: Selected Stories & Other Writings*. Ed. Donald Yates and James E. Irby. New York: New Directions, 1964.

PA *A Personal Anthology*. Ed. Anthony Kerrigan. New York: Grove Press, 1967.

S–P *Selected Poems*. Ed. Alexander Coleman. New York: Penguin, 1999.

SP *Selected Poems, 1923–1967*. Ed. Norman Thomas di Giovanni. New York: Delacorte Press, 1972.

PAUL DE MAN

A Modern Master

Although he has been writing poems, stories, and critical essays of the highest quality since 1923, the Argentinian writer Jorge Luis Borges is still much better known in Latin America than in the U. S. For the translator of John Peale Bishop. Hart Crane. E. E. Cummings. William Faulkner, Edgar Lee Masters, Robert Penn Warren, and Wallace Stevens, this neglect is somewhat unfair. There are signs however, that he is being discovered in this country with some of the same enthusiasm that greeted him in France, where he received major critical attention, and has been very well translated. Several volumes of translations in English have recently appeared, including a fine edition of his most recent book *El hacedor* (*Dreamtigers*)[1] and a new edition of *Labyrinths*, which first appeared in 1962. American and English critics have called him one of the greatest writers alive today, but have not as yet (so far as I know) made substantial contributions to the interpretation of his work. There are good reasons for this delay. Borges is a complex writer, particularly difficult to place. Commentators cast around in vain for suitable points of comparison and his own avowed literary admirations add to the confusion. Like Kafka and contemporary French existential writers, he is often seen as a moralist, in rebellion against the times. But such an approach is misleading.

From *New York Review of Books* 3, no. 6 (November 5, 1964). © 1964 by the Estate of Paul de Man. Reprinted by permission.

It is true that, especially in his earlier works, Borges writes about villains: The collection *History of Infamy* (*Historia universal de la infamia*, 1935) contains an engaging gallery of scoundrels. But Borges does not consider infamy primarily as a moral theme; the stories in no way suggest an indictment of society or of human nature or of destiny. Nor do they suggest the lighthearted view of Gide's Nietzschean hero Lafcadio. Instead, infamy functions here as an aesthetic, formal principle. The fictions literally could not have taken shape but for the presence of villainy at their very heart. Many different worlds are conjured up—cotton plantations along the Mississippi, pirate-infested South seas, the Wild West, the slums of New York, Japanese courts, the Arabian desert, etc.—all of which would be shapeless without the ordering presence of a villain at the center.

A good illustration can be taken from the imaginary essays on literary subjects that Borges was writing at the same time as the *History of Infamy*. Borrowing the stylistic conventions of scholarly critical writing, the essays read like a combination of Empson, Paulhan, and *PMLA*, except that they are a great deal more succinct and devious. In an essay on the translations of *The Thousand and One Nights*, Borges quotes an impressive list of examples showing how translator after translator mercilessly cut, expanded, distorted, and falsified the original in order to make it conform to his own and his audience's artistic and moral standards. The list, which amounts in fact to a full catalogue of human sins, culminates in the sterling character of Enna Littmann, whose 1923–1928 edition is scrupulously exact: "Incapable, like George Washington, of telling a lie, his work reveals nothing but German candor." This translation is vastly inferior, in Borges's eyes, to all others. It lacks the wealth of literary associations that allows the other, villainous translators to give their language depth, suggestiveness, ambiguity—in a word, style. The artist has to wear the mask of the villain or order to create a style.

So far, so good. All of us know that the poet is of the devil's party and that sin makes for better stories than virtue. It takes some effort to prefer *La nouvelle Héloise* to *Les liaisons dangereuses* or, for that matter, to prefer the second part of the *Nouvelle Héloise* to the first. Borges's theme of infamy could be just another form of *fin-de-siècle* aestheticism, a late gasp of romantic agony. Or, perhaps worse, he might be writing out of moral despair as an escape from the trappings of style. But such assumptions go against the grain of a writer whose commitment to style remains unshakable; whatever Borges's existential anxieties may be, they have little in common with Sartre's robustly prosaic view of literature, with the earnestness of Camus's moralism, or with the weighty profundity of German existential thought. Rather, they are the consistent expansion of a purely poetic consciousness to its furthest limits.

The stories that make up the bulk of Borges's literary work are not moral fables or parables like Kafka's, to which they are often misleadingly compared, even less attempts at psychological analysis. The least inadequate literary analogy would be with the eighteenth-century *conte philosophique*: their world is the representation, not of an actual experience, but of an intellectual proposition. One does not expect the same kind of psychological insight or the same immediacy of personal experience from *Candide* as from *Madame Bovary*, and Borges should be read with expectations closer to those one brings to Voltaire's tale than to a nineteenth-century novel. He differs, however, from his eighteenth-century antecedents in that the subject of the stories is the creation of style itself; in this Borges is very definitely postromantic and even post-symbolist. His main characters are prototypes for the writer, and his worlds are prototypes for a highly stylized kind of poetry or fiction. For all their variety of tone and setting, the different stories all have a similar point of departure, a similar structure, a similar climax, and a similar outcome; the inner cogency that links these four moments together constitutes Borges's distinctive style, as well as his comment upon this style. His stories are about the style in which they are written.

At their center, as I have said, always stands an act of infamy. The first story in *Labyrinths*, "Tlön, Uqbar, Orbis Tertius," describes the totally imaginary world of a fictitious planet; this world is first glimpsed in an encyclopedia which is itself a delinquent reprint of the *Britannica*. In "The Shape of the Sword," an ignominious Irishman who, as it turns out, betrayed the man who saved his life, passes himself off for his own victim in order to tell his story in a more interesting way. In "The Garden of the Forking Paths" the hero is a Chinese who, during World War I, spies on the British mostly for the satisfaction of refined labyrinthine dissimulation. All these crimes are misdeeds like plagiarism, impersonation, espionage, in which someone pretends to be what he is not, substitutes a misleading appearance for his actual being. One of the best of his early stories describes the exploits of the religious impostor

Hakim, who hides his face behind a mask of gold. Here the symbolic function of the villainous acts stands out very clearly: Hakim was at first a dyer, that is, someone who presents in bright and beautiful colors what was originally drab and gray. In this, he resembles the artist who confers irresistably attractive qualities upon something that does not necessarily possess them.

The creation of beauty thus begins as an act of duplicity. The writer engenders another self that is his mirror-like reversal. In this anti-self, the virtues and the vices of the original are curiously distorted and reversed. Borges describes the process poignantly in a later text called "Borges and I" (it appears in *Labyrinths* and also, in a somewhat better translation, in *Dreamtigers*). Although he is aware of the other Borges's "perverse habit of falsifying and exaggerating," he yields more and more to this poetic mask "who shares [his] preferences, but in a vain way that converts them into the attributes of an actor." This act, by which a man loses himself in the image he has created, is to Borges inseparable from poetic greatness. Cervantes achieved it when he invented and became Don Quixote; Valéry achieved it when he conceived and became Monsieur Teste. The duplicity of the artist, the grandeur as well as the misery of his calling, is a recurrent theme closely linked with the theme of infamy. Perhaps its fullest treatment appears in the story "Pierre Ménard, Author of the Quixote" in *Labyrinths*. The work and life of an imaginary writer is described by a devoted biographer. As the story unfolds, some of the details begin to have a familiar ring: even the phony, mercantile, snobbish Mediterranean atmosphere seems to recall to us an actual person, and when we are told that Ménard published an early sonnet in a magazine called *La conque*, a reader of Valéry will identify the model without fail. (Several of Valéry's early poems in fact appeared in *La conque*, which was edited by Pierre Louys, though at a somewhat earlier date than the one given by Borges for Ménard's first publication.) When, a little later, we find out that Ménard is the author of an invective against Paul Valéry, as well as the perpetrator of the shocking stylistic crime of transposing "*Le cimetière marin*" into alexandrines (Valéry has always insisted that the very essence of this famous poem resides in the decasyllabic meter), we can no longer doubt that we are dealing with Valéry's anti-self, in other words, Monsieur Teste. Things get a lot more complicated a few paragraphs later, when Ménard embarks on the curious project of re-inventing Don Quixote word for word, and by the time Borges treats us to a "close reading" of two identical passages from Don Quixote, one written by Cervantes, the other by Pierre Ménard (who is also Monsieur Teste, who is also Valéry) such a complex set of ironies, parodies, reflections, and issues are at play that no brief commentary can begin to do them justice.

Poetic invention begins in duplicity, but it does not stop there. For the writer's particular duplicity (the dyer's image in "Hakim") stems from the fact that he presents the invented form as if it possessed the attributes of reality, thus allowing it to be mimetically reproduced, in its turn, in another mirror-image that takes the preceding pseudo-reality for *its* starting-point. He is prompted "by the blasphemous intention of attributing the divine category of *being* to some mere [entities]". Consequently, the duplication grows into a proliferation of successive mirror-images. In "Tlön, Uqbar, Orbis Tertius," for example, the plagiarized encyclopedia is itself falsified by someone who adds an entry on the imaginary region Uqbar, presenting it as if it were part of an imaginary country as *his* starting point, another falsifier (who, by the way, is a Southern segregationist millionaire) conjures up, with the assistance of a team of shady experts, a complete encyclopedia of a fictional planet called Tlön—a pseudo-reality equal in size to our own real world. This edition will be followed in turn by a revised and even more detailed edition written not in English but in one of the languages of Tlön and entitled *Orbis Tertius*.

All the stories have a similar mirror-like structure, although the devices vary with diabolical ingenuity. Sometimes, there is only one mirror-effect, as when at the end of "The Shape of the Sword" Vincent Moon reveals his true identity as the villain, not the hero, of his own story. But in most of Borges's stories, there are several layers of reflection. In "Theme of the Traitor and the Hero" from *Labyrinths* we have: (1) an actual historic event—a revolutionary leader betrays his confederates and has to be executed; (2) a fictional story about such an occurrence (though in reversed form)—Shakespeare's *Julius Caesar*; (3) an actual historic event which copies the fiction: the execution is carried out according to Shakespeare's plot, to make sure that it will be a good show; (4) the puzzled historian reflecting on the odd alternation of identical fictional and historical events, and deriving a false theory of historical archetypes from them; (5) the smarter historian Borges (or, rather, his duplicitous antiself) reflecting on the credulous historian and reconstructing the true course of events. In other stories from *Labyrinths*, "The Immortal," "The Zahir," or "Death and the Compass," the complication is pushed so far that it is virtually impossible to describe.

This mirror-like proliferation constitutes, for Borges, an indication of poetic success. The works of literature he most admires contain this element; he is fascinated by such mirror-effects in literature as the Elizabethan play within the play, the character Don Quixote reading *Don Quixote*, Scheherazade beginning one night to retell *verbatim* the story of *The Thousand and One Nights*. For each mirrored image is stylistically superior to the preceding one, as the dyed cloth is more beautiful than the plain, the distorted translation richer than the original, Ménard's Quixote aesthetically more complex than Cervantes's. By carrying this process to its limits, the poet can achieve ultimate success—an ordered picture of reality that contains the totality of all things, subtly transformed and enriched by the imaginative process that engendered them. The imaginary world of Tlön is only one example of this poetic achievement; it recurs throughout Borges's work and constitutes, in fact, the central, climactic image around which each of the stories is organized. It can be the philosophically coherent set of laws that makes up the mental universe of Tlön, or it can be the fantastic world of a man blessed (as well as doomed) with the frightening gift of total recall, a man "who knows by heart the forms of the southern clouds at dawn on the 30th of April 1882" as well as "the stormy mane of a pony, the changing fire and its innumerable ashes" ("Funes the Memorious," in *Labyrinths*). It can be vastly expanded, like the infinitely complex labyrinth that is also an endless book in "The Garden of the Forking Paths," or highly compressed, like a certain spot in a certain house from which one can observe the entire universe ("The Aleph"), or a single coin which, however insignificant by itself, contains "universal history and the infinite concatenation of cause and effect" ("The Zahir"). All these points or domains of total vision symbolize the entirely successful and deceiving outcome of the poet's irrepressible urge for order.

The success of these poetic worlds is expressed by their all-inclusive and ordered wholeness. Their deceitful nature is harder to define, but essential to an understanding of Borges. Mirror images are indeed duplications of reality, but they change the temporal nature of this reality in an insidious fashion, even—one might say especially—

when the imitation is altogether successful (as in Ménard's Quixote). In actual experience, time appears to us as continuous but infinite; this continuity may seem reassuring, since it gives us some feeling of identity, but it is also terrifying, since it drags us irrevocably towards an unknowable future. Our "real" universe is like space: stable but chaotic. If, by an act of the mind comparable to Borges's will to style, we order this chaos, we may well succeed in achieving an order of sorts, but we dissolve the binding, spatial substance that held our chaotic universe together. Instead of an infinite mass of substance, we have a finite number of isolated events incapable of establishing relations among one another. The inhabitants of Borges's totally poetic world of Uqbar "do not conceive that the spatial persists in time. The perception of a cloud of smoke on the horizon and then of the burning field and then of the half-extinguished cigarette that produced the blaze is considered an example of association of ideas." This style in Borges becomes the ordering but dissolving act that transforms the unity of experience into the enumeration of its discontinuous parts. Hence his rejection of *style lié* and his preference for what grammarians call parataxis, the mere placing of events side by side, without conjunctions; hence also his definition of his own style as baroque, "the style that deliberately exhausts (or tries to exhaust) all its possibilities."[2] The style is a mirror, but unlike the mirror of the realists that never lets us forget for a moment that it creates what it mimics.

Probably because Borges is such a brilliant writer, his mirror-world is also profoundly, though always ironically, sinister. The shades of terror vary from the criminal gusto of the *History of Infamy* to the darker and shabbier world of the later *Ficciones*, and in *Dreamtigers* the violence is even starker and more somber, closer, I suppose, to the atmosphere of Borges's native Argentina. In the 1935 story, Hakim the impostor proclaimed: "The earth we live on is a mistake, a parody devoid of authority. Mirrors and paternity are abominable things, for they multiply this earth." This statement keeps recurring throughout the later work, but it becomes much more comprehensible there. Without ceasing to be the main metaphor for style, the mirror acquires deadly powers—a motif that runs throughout Western literature but of which Borges's version is particularly rich and complex. In his early work, the mirror of art represented the intention to keep the flow of time from losing itself forever in the shapeless void of infinity. Like the speculations of philosophers, style is an attempt at immortality. But this attempt is bound to fail. To quote one of Borges's favorite books, Sir Thomas Browne's *Hydrothapia, Urne-Buriall* (1658): "There is no antidote against the *Opium* of time, which temporally considereth all things ..." This is not, as has been said, because Borges's God plays the same trick on the poet that the poet plays on reality; God does not turn out to be the arch-villain set to deceive man into an illusion of eternity. The poetic impulse in all its perverse duplicity, belongs to man alone, marks him as essentially human. But God appears on the scene as the power of reality itself, in the form of a death that demonstrates the failure of poetry. This is the deeper reason for the violence that pervades all Borges's stories. God is on the side of chaotic reality and style is powerless to conquer him. His appearance is like the hideous face of Hakim when he loses the shining mask he has been wearing and reveals a face worn away by leprosy. The proliferation of mirrors is all the more terrifying because each new image brings us a step closer to this face.

As Borges grows older and his eyesight gets steadily weaker, this final confrontation throws its darkening shadow over his entire work, without however extinguishing the lucidity of his language. For although the last reflection may be the face of God himself, with his appearance the life of poetry comes to an end. The situation is very similar to that of Kierkegaard's aesthetic man, with the difference that Borges refuses to give up his poetic predicament for a leap into faith. This confers a somber glory on the pages of *Dreamtigers*, so different from the shining brilliance of the stories in *Labyrinths*. To understand the full complexity of this later mood, one must have followed Borges's enterprise from the start and see it as the unfolding of a poetic destiny. This would not only require the translation into English of Borges's earlier work, but also serious critical studies worthy of this great writer.

Notes

1. Other translations, aside from stories in anthologies or reviews, are to be found in *Ficciones*, edited by Anthony Kerrigan (New York: Grove Press, 1960). Bibliographical indications on the work of Borges, including mention of some critical studies, can be found in the New Directions volume *Labyrinths*. A much more extensive bibliography has just appeared in Paris, in the latest issue of *L'herne*, which is entirely devoted to Borges (Paris: *Lettres modernes*).

2. Prologue to the 1954 edition of *Universal History of Infamy*.

JAIME ALAZRAKI

Borges' modernism and the new critical idiom

In his essay on modern man, Jung has observed that although "many people call themselves modern—especially the pseudo-moderns—the really modern man is often to be found among those who call themselves *old fashioned*."[1] I doubt very much if Jung's category of modern man befits Borges. Writers like Musil, Beckett and Cortázar come much closer to this definition, even to the point of providing an illustration for Jung's profile of modern man. But I cannot think of anyone who has more strongly claimed to be old-fashioned and who has more consistently defended his right to be so than Borges. When asked about contemporary authors or more fashionable trends of thought, he has invariably replied that he "is not to blame if he was born in this century," adding: "Why should one pick his literary preferences from twentieth-century writers when one has thirty centuries of literature to choose." Supporting this seeming eccentricity, André Maurois has pointed out, rather hyperbolically, that "Borges has read everything, and especially what nobody reads anymore."[2] More recently, in William Buckley's interview, Borges has been held responsible for "reintroducing Americans to American writers," but to nineteenth-century American writers. "Borges reminds me"—writes Alfred Kazin—"not of contemporaries, not of any novelists, but of Poe and Melville, of Emerson and Thoreau, even to their 'immaturity'."[3] Being old-

From *Borges and the Kabbalah: And other essays on his fiction and poetry*. © 1988 by Cambridge University Press. Reprinted with the permission of Cambridge University Press.

fashioned in an age that worships contemporaneity is an expression of modernity, because, according to Jung, "to be 'unhistorical' is the Promethean sin, and in this sense the modern man is sinful."4

As for Borges, only when he stopped aping seventeenth-century Spanish writers, from Saavedra Fajardo to Quevedo and Gracián, did he begin to write the prose for which he is now known. He refers to those early years as his baroque period: "I used to write in a very baroque and ostentatious style. Out of timidity, I believed that if I wrote in a simple way, people would think that I did not know how to write. I felt then the need to prove that I knew many rare words and that I was able to combine them in a very startling fashion."5 Borges was then playing the role of being a modern writer, and by so doing he was, at most, a pseudo-modern. He was honoring a Spanish tradition against which he would eventually wage a fierce war, but even this was a form of attitudinizing. If "an honest admission of modernity means voluntarily declaring oneself bankrupt, taking the vows of poverty and chastity in a new sense, and—what is still more painful—renouncing the halo of sanctity which history bestows," as Jung has asserted, Borges' modernity as a writer begins with his own admission of the bankruptcy of the Spanish language (in his 1927 essay "The Language of Argentines"), with his acceptance of the poverty of literature as a whole, and with his acknowledgment that "perhaps universal history is the history of the diverse intonation of a few metaphors."6 The consequence of the first admission is the notion of style as "total efficiency and total invisibility," and the conclusion of the second, the idea that the writer's task is less to invent new metaphors than to rewrite old ones.

Borges was able to derive these two fundamental tenets only after he moved from a limited and provincial outlook on literature to a more cosmopolitan one. He remained old-fashioned in the sense that while reading Joyce he thought of Góngora, as he wrote in an essay of 1925,7 and while reading Kafka he was able to trace his precursors back to Zeno, Kierkegaard, Lord Dunsany, and Robert Browning.8 Borges resisted the dazzling and bewildering impressions that modern writers leave us with. Instead, he read them as updated versions of those few metaphors Homer coined once and for all. Raymond Queneau has said that "all literary work is either an *Iliad* or an *Odyssey*."9 Much earlier, Borges advanced a similar thesis: "The *Iliad*"—he wrote in *A History of Eternity*—"was composed some three thousand years ago; during this vast lapse of time every familiar and necessary affinity has been noted and recorded. This does not mean, of course, that the number of metaphors has been exhausted; the ways of stating or hinting at these hidden sympathies are, in fact, limitless."[10] Later, he will arrive at a conclusion which is a direct result of this early finding: "Perhaps it is a mistake to suppose that metaphors can be invented: the real ones, those that formulate intimate connections between one image and another, have always existed; those we can still invent are the false ones, which are not worth inventing."[11] Borges reads literature not as an archipelago of isolated texts, but as a written continent that comprises one single text. This holistic approach led him to the views of literature that form the backbone of his essay "The Flower of Coleridge," in which he quotes Valéry as saying that "the history of literature should not be the history of the authors and their work but rather the history of the Spirit," and refers to Shelley, who said that "all the poems of the past, present, and future are fragments of a single infinite poem."[12] The ultimate inference of this reasoning is the statement that "one literature differs from another not so much because of the text as for the manner in which it is read."[13] The writer's task is therefore to read anew those few metaphors, to rewrite, as Pierre Menard did, the *Quixote*, or as John Barth put it, referring to that story, "to write an original work of literature, the implicit theme of which is the difficulty, perhaps the unnecessity, of writing original works of literature."[14] Literature as a formal game? Literature as a verbal algebra? Literature as a mere syntax? Yes. Such is the sweeping conclusion that closes his short piece "Elementos de preceptiva": "Literature is fundamentally a syntactic fact."

That article was published in *Sur* in April 1933, the same year that most of the stories later to be collected in *A Universal History of Infamy* (1935) appeared in *Critica*. The two conclusions presented in the short note defined two basic elements of Borges' more mature concept of literature: first, the place and function of each word or group of words as the unit that conditions the effective or ineffective performance of a text, and therefore "the validity of rhetoric as a discipline of literary analysis"; and second, the formulation, in a nutshell, of a theory of literature which views writing as rewriting. I believe that Borges' modernity stems from these two main assumptions; one deals with language, and the other with syntax or structure as the text's basic raison d'être.

As early as 1927, Borges defined "total efficiency and total invisibility as the twin perfections of any style."[15] At the time he pronounced this dictum, it was only a desideratum, since he was still writing in the very Mannerist style he was castigating and rejecting. Only with the narratives of *A Universal History of Infamy* did he put this theoretical machinery to work. There are, of course, some differences between the prose style of *Inquisitions* (1925) and the prose of *The Language of Argentines* published three years later: fewer pompous words, showy neologisms, and tortuous constructions, but still a rather heavy and obtrusive prose. The last essay in the collection, the one that gives the title to the book, approaches the prose of the first essays of *Discusión* (1932), written in the late 1920s. It is not yet the compressed and free-flowing style of his more mature prose; there are still residues of the old style,[16] but one can easily notice a gradual cleansing of the baroque arabesques of his early writing. By 1933, the year of publication of the first stories of infamy, and in spite of what he later said in the preface to the collection ("The very title of these pages flaunts their baroque character"), he was able to write a more restrained, smooth, and balanced prose.[17]

The metaphysical perplexities of his later fiction are still missing in this collection, but one recognizes the basic traits of his masterful prose—a transparency one is tempted to call invisible, and, at the same time, the subtle use of a clockwork of stylistic devices. Five years after he defined what style ought to be, he produced a prose that was the skillful praxis of that earlier program.

The stories of infamy are also important on a different account. They represent the first instance in which Borges applied the literary strategy disclosed for the first time in the short note of 1933, namely that "literature is fundamentally a syntactic fact." In the preface to the 1954 edition of *A Universal History of Infamy*, he wrote: "These pages are the irresponsible game of a shy young man who dared not write stories and so amused himself by falsifying and distorting the tales of others."[18] Yet, the method of writing adopted in this first collection will become a permanent feature of his poetics of fiction in later collections. When he wrote the preface of 1954, he already knew, if one is to take his explanation at its face value, that he was going to remain *shy* for the rest of his literary career; but he turned his shyness into his most daring weapon. What he said about his tales of infamy applies to his entire narrative work. After *Ficciones* and *The Aleph*, he repeated, in the same apologetic tone of the 1954 preface, that he was rewriting what others had already written: "Everything I have written could be found in Poe, Stevenson, Wells, Chesterton, and some others."[19] One is tempted to dismiss this and similar declarations as sheer modesty, or perhaps false modesty. The truth is that the statement is neither literally accurate nor completely false; it is rather a casual formulation, with modesty as its dress, of what can be regarded as the cornerstone of his poetics. He is suggesting informally the same idea very carefully formulated in the essays quoted earlier, namely, writing as rewriting. Throughout prologues and comments, Borges will tirelessly restate this central notion. About the novel *The Approach to Almutasim*, that the story with the same title reviews, he said that it shows "the double tutelage of Wilkie Collins and of Farid ud-din Attar"; about "The Library of Babel" he wrote: "I am not the author of this narrative; those curious to know its history and its prehistory may interrogate a certain page of the 59th issue of the journal *Sur*, which records the heterogeneous names of Lecippus and Lasswitz, of Lewis Carroll and Aristotle" (*F*, 15). Of the "Circular Ruins," which is a recasting of the legend of the golem, he said: "Lewis Carroll gave me my epigraph, which may have been the story's seed" (*A*, 267). Of "Street-corner Man": "This story was written under the triple influence of Stevenson, G. K. Chesterton, and Josef von Sternberg's unforgettable gangster films" (*A*, 264). Of "Death and the Compass": "Should I add that the Hasidim included saints and that the sacrifice of four lives in order to obtain the four letters imposed by the Name is a fantasy which dictated the form of my story" (*F*, 105). Of "The Life of Tadeo Isidoro Cruz": "This tale is a gloss of the gaucho poem *Martín Fierro*, written by Hernández in 1872" (*A*, 270). Of "The End": "Apart from one character—Recabarren—nothing or almost nothing is an invention of mine; everything in it is implicit in a famous book, and I have merely been the first to reveal, or at least, to declare it" (*F*, 105). Of "Three Versions of Judas": "In this Christological fantasy I believe I perceive the remote influence of León Bloy" (*F*, 107). The postscript to "The Immortal" registers interpolations, intrusions or thefts from Pliny, De Quincey, Descartes, and Bernard Shaw, and Borges said of this story: "Blake wrote that if our senses did not work—if we were blind, deaf, etc.—we would see things as they are; infinite. "The Immortal" sprang from that strange idea and also from the verse by Rupert Brooke, "And see, no longer blinded by our eyes" (*A*, 279).

Of "The Dead Man": "Azevedo Bandeira, in that story, is a coarse divinity, a wild and mulatto version of Chesterton's incomparable Sunday (Chapter 29 of *Decline and Fall of the Roman Empire* tells a destiny similar to Otálora's but by far greater and more incredible)" (*A*, 271). Of "The Other Dead": "The eleventh-century churchman Pier Damiano grants God the unimaginable power of undoing the past. This idea gave me the start for my story" (*A*, 272).

One can find similar acknowledgments for most of his stories. It will be wrong to take them as demonstrations of sheer intellectual probity or mere modesty. They are of a piece with his proposition that literature is "the diverse intonations of a few metaphors" stated in a sketchy yet unequivocal way in the short note of 1933. In the "Afterword" for the English translation of *Doctor Brodie's Report*, he reiterates: "William Morris thought that the essential stories of man's imagination had long since been told and that by now the storyteller's craft lay in rethinking and retelling them ... I do not go as far as Morris went, but to me the writing of a story has more of a discovery about it than of deliberate invention." (*DBR*, 123)

Unknowingly, Borges was placing himself at the very center of one of the most modern approaches to literary theory. The Russian Formalists strove to define literature in terms similar to the ones enunciated by Borges. They believed that texts are not born in a vacuum, but evolve from other texts. What changes is less the ideas elicited by them than the new syntax that governs the rewriting of the old text. Eichenbaum, for instance, found that Tolstoy created the new Russian novel following the direct legacy of the eighteenth-century novel; Osip Brik ascertained that the vaudeville writer Belopiatkin was reborn in Nekrasov. They also concluded that Blok canonized the themes and rhythms of the "Gypsy Song," that Chekhov bestowed literary status to the *Budilnik*, a comic newspaper in nineteenth-century Russia, and that Dostoevski brought to his works the devices of the dime novel.[20] Their overall conclusion was that "new forms come about not in order to express new contents but in order to replace old forms."[21] Viktor Shklovsky, in his essay "Art as Artifice," gives further and rather surprising support to Borges' own outlook on literature as "the diverse intonations of a few metaphors." Shklovsky's comment sounds like a paraphrase of Borges' notion: "Images"—he says—"originate nowhere, they belong to God. The more one gets to know a period, the more one is persuaded that those images that were considered as a creation of this or that poet, were taken by him from another poet almost without any modification. The task of poetic schools is no other than the accumulation and revelation of new devices for *disposing* and elaborating the verbal material, and it consists in the *disposition* of the images rather than in their creation. Images are there, once and for all, and in poetry they are remembered rather than utilized for thinking."[22] Although Shklovsky's article was published as early as 1917, it is most unlikely that Borges knew it. The doctrine of the Formalists was not known in Western Europe until the 1940s, when Jakobson moved to the United States and one of his students, Victor Erlich, published in 1955 the first book-length survey of the movement. One is forced to conclude that Borges was working on his own, and that he arrived independently at conclusions similar to those reached by the Formalists. Besides, critical theory was for him a subsidiary undertaking intended to sharpen his own awareness as a writer. He did what the Formalists did not do: he incorporated some of his ideas about literature into his creative writing, thus amalgamating theory and craft.

If one thinks of French structuralism as a consequence and derivation of Russian formalism—and Lévi-Strauss was the first to acknowledge the debt of his anthropology to Vladimir Propp and the members of the *Opoiiaz*—it is understandable that Borges' notion of literature as syntax overlapped with the structuralist concept of literature as a system (Barthes). It is also understandable that a structuralist critic such as Gérard Genette should read Borges with so much fascination and conviction. Genette echoed Borges' enthusiasm for the idea of all literature constituting a single text, and relying on this assumption proposed the following definition: "Literature is a coherent whole, a congruous space in whose interior the works touch and penetrate each other."[23] He further supported his definition with the notion of writing as rewriting developed by Borges in the essay "For Bernard Shaw" where he wrote: "If I were to read any contemporary page as it would be read in the year 2000, I would know what the literature would be like in the year 2000" (*OI*, 173). Genette quotes this sentence as the foundation for a structuralist theory of literature.

In the first part of "Elementos de preceptiva," Borges undertakes the stylistic examination of a *milonga* discovered "in a rural grocery store near Arapey, at the beginning of 1931." He leaves to Spitzer, he says, "las vivencias originales que la determinaron;" he simply seeks to explore its verbal effectiveness. What this example shows, Borges concludes, together with the analysis of two lines from the tango *Villa Crespo*, is that "a subtle interplay of changes, clever frustrations and supports defines the aesthetic artifact; those who neglect or ignore it, ignore literature's raison d'être."[24] Borges was showing in 1933 that poetic functions are not exclusive attributes of literary texts; they can appear in a *milonga* or a tango, or even in an anonymous inscription written on a street wall.

Roman Jakobson will say and do something similar in 1960. To prove that "the linguistic study of the poetic function must overstep the limits of poetry,"[25] he examined the various phonetic and morphological functions operating in the structural system of the election slogan, "I like Ike." For Jakobson, poetics, as the discipline that deals with problems of verbal structure, sees literature much as Borges did in 1933, as a syntactic construct. In the same essay, Jakobson warned that "the terminological confusion of 'literary studies' with 'criticism' tempts the student of literature to replace the description of intrinsic values of literary works by a subjective, censorious verdict."[26] Borges voiced, at the conclusion of his 1933 short note, a similar warning: "If there is no single word written in vain, if even a popular *milonga* is a world of attractions and rejections, how to elucidate the 1056 quarto-pages attributed to a Shakespeare? How to take seriously those who judge them as a whole, without any method other than a loud emission of terrifying praises, and without examining a single line?"[27]

Finally, I would like to add that when Borges postulated in 1927 "total invisibility and total effectiveness as the twin perfections of any style," he was anticipating Camus by twenty-four years. It was not until 1951 when the author of *The Rebel* wrote that "great style is invisible stylization, or rather stylization incarnate."[28] Two years later, Roland Barthes studied this trend against artistry in contemporary French fiction and coined the formula "writing degree zero." What he said in his essay was a restatement and a development of Camus' basic point: "This neutral writing achieves a style of absence which is almost an ideal absence of style ...; it deliberately foregoes any elegance or ornament; it is the mode of a new situation of the writer, the way a certain silence has of existing."[29] More straightforward, more matter-of-fact, Borges had been saying the same in the 1920s, and had been putting this principle to work in his own writing since the 1930s. But Borges lived in Buenos

Aires, not in Paris, and he was an Argentine who did not have the prestige and the weight of a literature which, like the French, had been dominating the European literary scene since the eighteenth century. Recognition came late, but the seed of Borges' modernity was already implanted in his early writing.

When Borges' work was translated into most European languages and became better known in Europe and the United States, his fiction and essays became a driving force in modern letters. Some critics have seen Borges' place in contemporary literature as a new example which "served to release the influence of others, including his own master, Kafka, and even such different writers as Beckett and Robbe-Grillet."[30] More germane to our topic is the fact that one of the most recent approaches to have appeared in the critical arena, after structuralism, found its spokesman in Borges. I am referring to intertextuality. Borges wrote the story that became the metaphor and the credo of the new method—"Pierre Menard, Author of the *Quixote*." In addition, at about the same time he wrote "Elements of Rhetoric" he published his first collection of short stories—*A Universal History of Infamy* (1935)—and in the preface strongly stated that he was not the author of those stories but merely their counterfeiter; he meant that he rewrote stories already written by others. Yet this "game of a shy man who dared not to write his own stories"[31] became his strongest asset. Borges turned his "shyness" into a powerful literary weapon by holding that writing is inevitably rewriting. Intertextuality is—in oversimplified terms—the study of the relationships between two or more texts, one that functions as a model or "hypotext" and a second or "hypertext" whose production is based on the first. The most important book on the method to have appeared so far is Gérard Genette's *Palimpsestes: La Littérature au second degré* (Paris, 1982). Genette borrowed the title from a passage in "Pierre Menard, Author. of the *Quixote*."[32] and there is even an indirect acknowledgment (p. 452). The debt to Borges is further recognized throughout Genette's book. Here he defines what the method owes to Borges:

> Attribuant à d'autres l'invention de ses contes, Borges présente au contraire son écriture comme une lecture considérée comme, ou déguisée en lecture son écriture. Ces deux conduites, faut-il le dire, sont complémentaires, elles s'unissent en une métaphore des relations, complexes et

ambiguës, de l'écriture et de la lecture: relations qui sont bien évidemment—j'y reviendrai s'il le faut—l'âime même de l'activité hypertextuelle.[33]

Borges always had a keen interest in and a strong attraction to the classics.[34] After his brief participation in the Spanish brand of the avant-garde—*ultraísmo*—and later in his more mature period, he gave blunt signs of impatience toward modern writers. If as early as 1925 he translated into Spanish "the last page" of Joyce's *Ulysses*, from the late fifties on—as his blindness became more advanced—he turned more and more toward the past: he began the study of Old English and Old Norse, returned to his favorite Victorian writers, kept rereading the classics, and became disdainful and even vitriolic about the moderns. He did his best to be seen and known as old-fashioned. Ironically, he became not only "a classic of modern fiction," as John Barth defined him, but also the guru of modern literary perception.

NOTES

1. Carl G. Jung, "The Spiritual Problem of Modern Man." *The Portable Jung*, edited by Joseph Campbell. New York, Viking, 1971, p. 459.

2. André Maurois, "Preface" to *Labyrinths: Selected Stories and Other Writings*, edited by D. A. Yates & J. E. Irby. New York, New Directions, 1964, p. ix.

3. Alfred Kazin, "Meeting Borges," *The New York Times Book Review*, May 2, 1971, p. 5.

4. Carl G. Jung, *op. cit.*, p. 458.

5. James E. Irby, "Encuentro con Borges." *Vida universitaria*, Monterrey, Mexico, April 12, 1964, p. 14 (my translation).

6. Borges. *OI*, 8.

7. Borges, "El *Ulises* de Joyce," *I*, 25.

8. Borges, "Kafka and His Precursors," *OI*, 111–113.

9. Quoted by Gérard Genette in *Figuras; retórica y estructuralismo*. Cordoba (Argentina), Nagelkop, 1970, p. 187.

10. Borges, *HE*, 74.

11. Borges, *OI*, 47.

12. *Ibid.*, p. 9.

13. *Ibid.*, p. 173.

14. John Barth, "The Literature of Exhaustion." *The Atlantic*, August 1961, p. 31.

15. Jorge Luis Borges, "Eduardo Wilde," *IA*, 158.

16. See the following paragraphs extracted from his essay "La penúltima versión de la realidad" of 1928 and included in *Discusión*: "Gaspar Marin, que ejerce la metafísica en Buenos Aires.... Creo delusoria la oposición entre los dos conceptos incontrastables de espacio y de tiempo. Me consta que la genealogía de esa equivocación es ilustre ... Quiero complementar esas dos imaginaciones ilustres con una mía, que es derivación y facilitación." (*D*, 42–44)

17. If those pages could be called Baroque they are so only in the sense defined by John Barth: "While his own work *is not* Baroque, except intellectually (the Baroque was never so terse, laconic, economical), it suggests the view that intellectual and literary history has been Baroque, and has pretty well exhausted the possibilities of novelty" (Barth, *op. cit.*, p. 34).

As an example of this new, more tempered prose, read this passage from "El espantoso redentor Lazarus Morell"; "A principios del siglo diecinueve las vastas plantaciones de algodón que labía en las orillas eran trabajadas por negros, de sol a sol. Dormían en cabañas de madera, sobre el piso de tierra. Fuera de la relación madre-hijo, los parentescos eran convencionales y turbios. Nombres tenían, pero podían prescindir de apellidos. No sabían leer" (*HU*, 19).

18. Borges, *Historia Universal*, p. 10 (translation by Norman T. di Giovanni, "Preface to *A Universal History of Infamy*" in *Prose for Borges*, by Mary Kinzie, *TriQuarterly*, No. 25, Fall 1972, p. 203).

19. J. Irby, N. Murat, & C. Peralta, *Encuentro con Borges*. Buenos Aires, Galerna, 1968, pp. 37–38.

20. See L. Matejka & K. Pomorska, eds., *Readings in Russian Poetics; Formalist and Structuralist Views*. MIT Press, 1971, p. 32.

21. *Ibid.*, p. 29.

22. Tzvetan Todorov, ed., *Teoría de la literatura de los formalistas rusos*. Buenos Aires, Signos, 1970, p. 56 (my translation).

23. Gérard Genette, *op. cit.*, p. 186 (my translation).

24. Jorge Luis Borges, "Elementos de preceptiva." *Sur*, año III, No. 7, abril de 1933, p. 159 (my translation).

25. Roman Jakobson, "Linguistics and Poetics." *Style in Language*, edited by Thomas A. Sebeok. MIT Press, 1960, p. 357.

26. *Ibid.*, pp. 351–352.

27. Borges, "Elementos de preceptiva", p. 161. (my translation).

28. Albert Camus, *The Rebel*. New York, 1961, pp. 271–272.

29. Roland Barthes, *Writing Degree Zero*. London, 1967, pp. 83–84. (First published in 1953 as *Le degré zéro de L'écriture*.)

30. Morris Dickstein, *The New York Times Book Review*, April 26, 1970.

31. Jorge Luis Borges, *A Universal History Infamy*. New York, Dutton, 1979, p. 12 (*UH*, 12).

32. In that passage, Borges writes: "I have reflected that it is permissible to see in this 'final' *Quixote* a kind of palimpsest, through which the traces—tenuous but not indecipherable—of our friend's 'previous' writing should be translucently visible." *Labyrinths; Selected Stories and Other Writings*. New York, New Directions, 1964, p. 44. (*L*, 44)

33. Gérard Genette, *Palimpsestes. La littérature au second degré*. Paris, Seuil, 1982, p. 296.

34. See his essay "Sobre los clásicos" in *Sur* (Buenos Aires, Oct., 1941, No. 85), pp. 7–12.

Abbreviations

A	*The Aleph and Other Stories, 1933–1969*. Ed. and trans. by Norman Thomas di Giovanni in collaboration with the author. New York: E. P. Dutton, 1970.
BIB	*The Book of Imaginary Beings* (translated by N.T. di Giovanni in collaboration with the author). New York: Avon Books, 1970.
C	*La cifra*. Buenos Aires: Emecé, 1981.
D	*Discusión*. Buenos Aires: Emecé, 1964.
DBR	*Doctor Brodie's Report* (translated by N.T. di Giovanni in collaboration with the author). New York: E.P. Dutton, 1972.
DT	*Dreamtigers* (translated by M. Boyer and H. Morland). Austin: University of Texas Press, 1968.
ES	*Elogio de la sombra*. Buenos Aires: Emecé, 1969.
F	*Ficciones* (edited by A. Kerrigan). New York: Grove Press, 1962.
GT	*The Gold of the Tigers* (translated by Alistair Reid). New York: E.P. Dutton, 1977.
HE	*Historia de la eternidad*. Buenos Aires: Emecé: 1961.
HN	*Historia universal de la infamia*. Buenos Aires Emecé, 1962.
I	*Inquisiciones*. Buenos Aires: Proa, 1925.
IA	*El idioma de los argentinos*. Buenos Aires: Gleizer, 1928.
L	*Labyrinths: Selected Stories & Other Writings*. Ed. Donald Yates and James E. Irby. New York: New Directions, 1964.
MEP	*Modern European Poetry* (edited by W. Barnstone et al.). New York: Bantam. 1978.

MARÍA ROSA MENOCAL

Blindness: Alephs and Lovers

> *Era inevitable: el olor de las almendras amargas le recordaba siempre el destino de los amores contrariados.*
>
> It was inevitable: the scent of bitter almonds always reminded him of the fate of unrequited love.
>
> "*Y hasta cuándo cree usted que podemos seguir en este ir y venir del carajo?*" *le preguntó.*
> *Florentino Ariza tenía la respuesta preparada desde hacía cincuenta y tres años, siete meses y once días con sus noches.*
> "*Toda la vida*" *dijo.*
>
> "And how long do you think we can keep up this goddamn coming and going?" he asked.
> Florentino Ariza had kept his answer ready for fifty-three years, seven months, and eleven days and nights.
> "Forever," he said.
> —Gabriel García Márquez, *El amor en los tiempos del cólera*, translated by Edith Grossman

I

Jorge Luis Borges begins the last of his nine essays on Dante with the arresting line "Mi propósito es comentar los versos más patéticos que la

---

From *Writing in Dante's Cult of Truth From Borges to Boccaccio.* © 1991 by Duke University Press. Reprinted by permission.

literatura ha alcanzado" (155) (My purpose is to comment on the most moving and plaintive lines in literature).[1] The pathos that has left Borges so clearly affected—and that in some ways in Borges's recounting is far more passionate than we are used to reading in Dante himself—is not only that Dante's mortal, earthly, "real" love was unrequited and tragic, but that even in fiction, a monumental fiction constructed precisely so that he could meet the vanished Beatrice once again, Dante could not fully falsify matters, could not be glaringly untrue to the earthly truth that had so scarred and shaped him. Thus, his argument goes (here and in the previous essay, also devoted to the figure, the persona, of Beatrice), Dante could not quite make her nice, could not so transfigure a transcendent truth, the transcendent truth that she had never loved him, and make her do all those things that in his heart of hearts he no doubt wanted—most of all, of course, to have her love him as he had her. Dante has been trapped and tricked by his own belief in Truth.

It is not surprising that this same Dante, Borges's Dante, would damn the most marvelous of his creatures, Francesca, a Francesca who flaunts a wildly passionate, requited love in the poor Pilgrim's face, a Francesca who cannot help but rub it in by using the *noi* form, who does not, cannot, of course, regret her love because it is what she is. Borges is quick to point out that after her first narration all Dante really wants to know from her is how and when they, the lovers, knew that they were, in fact, in love with each other, mortal and mortally dangerous love, and it is precisely that question that provokes the second part of Francesca's lovely recounting of the book and the kiss. This Dante is not impervious to envy, at least a slight tremor of it, and while Borges is at pains to point out, to say out loud, that Dante does not (mis)use his powers to condemn and save for petty or personal reasons, one is left, in the aftermath, with a slightly bad taste in one's mouth: could he really have resented passionately requited love, the fulfilling embrace, so much? His Beatrice seems everywhere, alive or dead, incapable of such passion, seems, indeed, to be the serenity that comes outside such passion, only in its wake or absence, and in Dante's terms it is a true love that transcends— and ultimately negates, explicitly—the kind of passion that the whirling dervish Francesca embodies.

But after the simplicity, that simple lovingness and sentimentality of Borges's reading settles in, after we realize that this, after all, is why his Beatriz is but a portrait hanging on a wall (not that she would be a dead woman—that much we understood—but a portrait that smells of dust and cold), after all this there remains the simple but compelling question: why did he have to make her that way? Why can Dante, in his remarkable literary prowess and in the midst of a monument erected precisely so he could meet up with her once more, not make Beatrice cherish and love him, even, if he so wished and willed it, be passionately and madly in love with him? Borges's answer to his own implicit question is at first glance either lame or disingenuous: because he had to remain true to the historical truth. Coming from a writer dedicated to dismantling the epistemological divisions between literary truth and other truths—and written about the author of a magic text such as the *Vita nuova*—it is an argument that on the face of it seems to melt away when you pour water on it.

Or perhaps it is simply Borges's way of signalling and repeating a very "Dantesque" lesson about the reading of texts: that the Truth is there, in the text, but only if we are able to believe in it. Borges's momentary play at the pseudonaive reader—clearly a role he cherishes—lets us see the more important truth uncovered by his apparently simple reading: that, because History and Truth and Text coincide, Beatrice must be precisely what she is. What Dante knows, and only momentarily regrets in that second circle of Hell, is precisely what he traced out in the *Vita nuova*: that writing passionate love is, like physical passion itself, only a temporary and evanescent revelation, whereas even the pain in writing a love like Beatrice is transcendently powerful, True. Borges the reader, who talks about the "truth" of historical events and who sheds tears at the pathos of Beatrice's last smile, is speaking as one who doesn't quite believe in the truth of the matter. He knows too well that the *Commedia* is a text that cultivates total vision and total engagement with the Truth—and that Dante's notion of the Truth is infinitely beyond the more banal one of personal history. But, writing passionately as the innocent reader, Borges doesn't quite buy it. What better criticism, finally, of Dante's logology—celebrated elsewhere by Borges the admirer of Dante[2]—than Borges's suggestion that in the end, at the summit of Dante's creation, literally, she had to be as distant as she had been in life, because Dante could not break from the mold, could not invent something richer. Beatriz is the dead woman, a dusty portrait hanging in darkened, chilly rooms that are going to be demolished. Truth is the Aleph, the magic shown to the faintly ridiculous Daneri, who doesn't really know the true magic of poetry.

Before Borges, only Petrarch managed an equally coy and devastating reading. And as in the case of Borges (or for that matter, in the case of Dante himself, with respect to Arnaut), it is the sort of love–hate relationship that throws off sparks of resentment as easily as it does the flattery of imitation, the reverence of certain kinds of acknowledgment. And what Borges never said was whether the different pictures of Beatriz vanished in the same dust as the demolished house— and the Aleph in the basement—or was dragged off to a new home by a Daneri who by then had used the Aleph for what it was worth to him, to win his literary prize. The portrait, at any rate, is never seen again.

II

Chi è questa che vèn, ch'ogn'om la mira,
e fa tremar di chiaritate l'are,
e mena seco Amor, sì che parlare
null'omo pote, ma ciascun sospira?

O Deo che sembra quando li occhi gira
dical'Amor, chi'i' nol savria contare:
cotanto d'umilta donna mi pare
che ogn'altra inver' di lei la chiam'ira

Non si porìa contar la sua piagenza,
ch'a le' s'inchin' ogni gentil vertute,
e la beltate per sua dea la mostra

Non fu sì alta già la mente nostra,
e non si pose in not tanta salute,
che propriamente n'avrian canoscenza

Who is she who comes, that everyone looks at her,
Who makes the air tremble with clarity
And brings Love with her, so that no one
Can speak, though everyone sighs?

> O God, what she looks like when she turns her eyes
> Let Love say, for I could not describe it.
> To me she seems so much a lady of good will
> That any other, in comparison to her, I call vexation.
>
> One could not describe her gracefulness,
> for every noble virtue inclines towards her
> And beauty displays her as its goddess.
>
> Our mind was never so lofty
> And never was such beatitude granted us
> That we could really have knowledge of her.
> (*The Poetry of Guido Cavalcanti*,
> trans. Lowry Nelson, Jr., 6–7)

No poet can have had a relationship with Dante at once so painfully and nakedly neurotic and, in terms of the posterity that obsessed the later poet, so successful as Petrarch. Petrarch is a Borgesian reader: as with Borges's famous observations, most succinctly enunciated in his essay on Kafka, Petrarch deftly creates his own precursors, writes anew for us his literary ancestry, from the Augustan poets to, most conspicuously, Dante himself. The *Rime sparse*[3] achieves among other things precisely what Borges suggests the successful epigone will manage: to make us read the "original," the precursors, in a different way. A recent study rather neatly points out that in this scheme of things Borges has deftly inverted the usual order of poetic obligation, for now the precursor owes a debt to the epigone, for the latter has caused the former to be read anew.[4]

But this presumes innocence, of course, of which there can be precious little in literary relations: if nothing else, already inscribed within Borges's reading itself, and within virtually any theory of reading beyond the most naive, there can be no "innocent" reading, far less any pure or "faithful" rewriting, even when that is the apparent, perhaps even conscious intent. But most precursors would have little to be grateful for in the inventions, the readings and writings, of their epigones, particularly those most richly talented, most frequently read (and thus, presumably, with the greatest press). For it is not the malformation of the new poet, in the Bloomian frame of analysis, that is at stake and to be feared. Rather, understanding the radically adiachronic nature of literary history, it is the interpretation of the earlier poet, potentially supreme in its influence, by those unborn, by the unknowable future, that critically affects and effectively writes the course of literary history. And it is a literary history, as I have discussed in the previous chapter, that until relatively recently was not written by the "professional" literary historians but by the critical readings, either direct or inscribed in their own poetry, of later generations of poets. In these terms Borges and Petrarch are allies and contemporaries, part of the same chapter in a synchronistic history: they would have us read Dante in very much the same way. And, inevitably, their reading of the precursor that the one cannot name and the other names and names and names into a kind of banality tells us at least as much, probably more about themselves. And that, of course, is exactly as things are supposed to turn out.

Petrarch's rather tortuous relationship with a Dante who, already in Petrarch's lifetime, was casting a long and seemingly impenetrable shadow over all poetry has been dealt with at some length and from a number of perspectives, although, as in other related matters, the strength of Petrarch's own dicta on the subject have had a surprisingly powerful effect.[5] And Petrarch's stated position on the subject, neatly set out to Boccaccio (the one other individual from whom Petrarch logically enough assumed he would have sufficient empathy and sympathy to fully understand) was that he, Petrarch, had never read Dante, precisely in order to avoid the kind of "influence" future readers would certainly seek and find.[6] Petrarch, at least, knows he must struggle to write not only the poetry but that poetry's own future history. Crucially, he knows he has the power to write another poet's history, without ever even naming him.

Multiple ironies abound, none more significant, perhaps, than that the poets whose "influence" Petrarch not only acknowledges but cultivates are far from the center of his attention, that center where Dante, or more precisely a refutation of Dante, resides. And it is no less ironic, perhaps, that in this way Petrarch's stated view is accurate even if it is false: the kind of "influence" that Dante has on him cannot be measured in the same terms as any or all of the other "precursors" openly inscribed in his works. With Dante, read but indeed not read and studied like the others at all, the relationship is paradigmatically

Borgesian: he will give us a reading of this "precursor" that we will not be able to fully escape, he will write some of the parameters of literary history for us—and he will do it all with scarcely a whisper of the other's name. That is the price of earlier fame and the vulgarity and popularity Petrarch both criticizes and envies in Dante and covets and fears for himself: the *Commedia* is public property and public knowledge, and Petrarch can come along and, in the utter discretion needed to salvage dignity and propriety and obscure all indications of envy, tell us just what is wrong with it—and why the *Rime sparse* are, ultimately, better poetry. Borges can have only pretended that these ancestral relationships were even remotely innocent; it is the same pretense one can hear on Petrarch's lips in that famous letter to Boccaccio, it is the pretense we hear on every page of "The Aleph," where Borges himself, in full "innocence," gives a version of Dante, an ancestor he elsewhere reveres, that is powerfully unreverential.

I make no attempt at a comprehensive view of either epigone's relationship with the Dante he battles on so many pages, nor am I interested in those relationships for the light—the "influence"—possibly shed on the later poet. These are other subjects, and they are treated, at least in part, by other critics. The far more restricted subject of my attention is the one Borges and Petrarch cry out to have examined: the influence they have on Dante, how they have cajoled and coerced and poeticized us into reading him, how they shape him. And why the blind Argentine and the probably insufferable, wandering half-Avignonais, half-Florentine should have so closely shared a vision of their elder is the delicious question that emerges forcefully, and is probably doomed to lie, at best, half-answered.

III

Lasso me, ch'i' non so in qual parte pieghi
la speme ch'è tradita omai più volte!
Che se non è chi con pietà m'ascolte,
perché sparger al ciel sì spessi preghi?
Ma s'egli aven ch'ancor non mi si nieghi
finir anzi 'l mio fine
queste voci meschine,
non gravi al mio signor perch'io il ripreghi

di dir libero un dì tra l'erba e i fiori:
"drez et rayson es qu'ieu ciant em demori."

Alas I do not know where to turn the hope that has been by now betrayed many times! For if there is no one who will listen to me with pity, why scatter prayers to the heavens so thickly? But if it happens that I am not denied the ending of these pitiful sounds before my death, let it not displease my lord that I beg him again to let me say freely one day among the grass and flowers: "It is right and just that I sing and be joyful." (This and subsequent citations from Petrarca, *Petrarch's Lyric Poems*, trans. Robert M. Durling, 150–51)

Arnaut Daniel has come back to life. He has beaten his way back from those purifying flames that made him spout that crystal-clear Provençal, doing, no, saying penance for so much poetic sin in his past. And he has come back not only to take back that repentance but to beg for the chance to do it again, to beg to be allowed to be free merely to sing, as he once did, before being locked up in a Purgatory that asked of him much more than mere happiness and singing. Arnaut is back with a vengeance here: his is not only the last line but the general structure of the entire poem, *canzone* 80, technically readable as a *sestina*—that seductively difficult form whose invention made Arnaut (in)famous.[7] Even more: in this tour de force of poetic imitation and commentary, with each stanza recasting the poetics of a different predecessor and finishing with a direct quotation from that poet, Petrarch does homage to Arnaut even in the Dante stanza. After Petrarch has given voices to Arnaut and to Guido Cavalcanti (another poet with whom the reprimanded Arnaut might have felt some kinship, another of Dante's "victims"), Dante's stanza is a recasting of one of the *petrose*, those spectacular odes to the virtuosity and hermeticism of Arnaut that Dante had once written but, of course, repented of.

Petrarch's Arnaut of that first stanza, which opens with a "Lasso me" that ties him to the most conventional of the love plaints of the Provençal lyric—and, equally, is the first of many hints that this Arnaut knows his fate lies with Dante—is engaged in a stark defense of his own poetics. Like the converted Arnaut created by Dante, he has forsaken the striking hermeticism that made his name. Here, however, it is to do battle, a battle over his own poetics, with that other Arnaut of the *Purgatorio*. He has almost given up, he has almost yielded to the (once again Borgesian) fate of having Dante rewrite and seal his poetics for posterity, and give him a place in literary history that is false. But hope is momentarily restored, a new epigone and historian comes along, and it would appear that he will not be "denied these pitiful sounds before my death." Petrarch's choice of verse in Provençal to have his reinvented and revivified Arnaut recite is a curious case of a false attribution contextually working as well as or even better than any "authentic" verse of Arnaut's might have: again, a limpid style stands in place of that Pound-like difficulty that was the real Arnaut's. In this particular poetic instance—Petrarch's battle with Dante over the validity and merits of the poetics of the *trobar clus*—the arrow-straight statement of the "simple" joys of "carefree" verse serves the rhetorical purpose best. The falsely attributed verse, ironically, expresses that most fundamental aspect of the value of lyrical language as well as many of Arnaut's own, and better (certainly more directly) than most of his more famous verses. And the Petrarchan verses that introduce Arnaut—an Arnaut whose soul speaks Italian before he sings in the Provençal of his youth—carefully construct an impeccably simple scene for that reprisal of that much-desired singing itself, "tra l'erba e i fiori" (among the grass and flowers). The simple joys of song are "just and right" in and of themselves, as "meaningful" (or not) as the grass and flowers themselves.

    The rehabilitation of Arnaut is given a broader frame of reference than the single, particular poet: Petrarch knows full well that what is at stake is more than Arnaut Daniel pure and simple, both for Dante and, in reprising the battle, for himself. The abundance of allusions to a discarded past for which the poet yearns ("omai piú volte," "ancor ... anzi 'l mio fine," "perch'io il ripieghi ... un dí ...") dovetails perfectly with the extensive and often diffuse thematics of memory that permeate, for some even dominate, the *Rime sparse*.[8] But in this particular case, at least, where the metaliterary and the metaliterary-historical issues are so unambiguously at the surface, that past is at the same time the very specific poetic past that precedes Dante himself, and Dante's rewriting of it. For if Petrarch is engaged in this Borgesian creation of a literary history, he is doing so in silent but unmistakable response to the literary historian who precedes him—Dante. Dante, in turn, like Petrarch himself, is a historian aware that what is at stake is the future and its readings. And we see here a characteristic example of Petrarch's most fundamental strategy, that "genius" that will allow him to battle Dante most effectively: he makes unmistakable reference to the rival ideology but never graces it with much beyond the necessary allusion, is never trapped into the obeisance and reverence and acquiescence of more extensive imitation. Petrarch is battling for the supremacy of lyric, and he will wage his battle in its fragmented and allusive and ambiguous tones: the Arnaut of a half-canto, the Arnaut of three full *terzine* in Provençal, is here come and gone with one stanza where he is half himself and half Petrarch, a purposefully ambiguous "I" that suggests the merger of advocacy of a good trial lawyer—and one fleeting verse in Provençal. Petrarch is taunting Dante with the spareness of his lyric and, a bit more disingenuously, with the innocence and purity and unencumbered value of song itself. Just as Petrarch is pleading not only his own case but Arnaut's, Arnaut/Petrarch is pleading the case of lyric poetry before Dante and Dante's revisions to literary history, and, most crucially, lyric poetry after Dante. In this version of the story, a version set to stand as a rival to that of the *Vita nuova* and the cantos of the *Commedia* that pursue and fill out the argument, the creative freedom from the external ideology and its manifold constraints of the love lyric is the response to Dante's charge of solipsism: the poet otherwise constrained is gagged, muted, infertile. And value? The lyric, the song, the sounds that may or may not make sense—sense being an ideological construct, after all—are themselves and in and of themselves meaningful, as much as their setting, "tra l'erba e i fiori."

> Ragion á ben ch'alcuna volta io canti
> pero ch' ò sospirato sì gran tempo
> che mai non incomincio assai per tempo
> per adequar col riso i dolor tanti.
> Et s'io potesse far ch'agli occhi santi
> porgesse alcun diletto
> qualche dolce mio detto,
> o me beato sopra gli amanti!
> Ma più quand'io dirò senza mentire:
> "Donna mi priega, per ch'io voglio dire."

It is just that at some time I sing, since I have sighed for so long a time that I shall never begin soon enough to make my smiling equal so many sorrows. And if I could make some sweet saying of mine give some delight to those holy eyes, oh me blessed above other lovers! But most when I can say without lying: "A lady begs me; therefore I wish to speak."

The second rehabilitation and rewriting: the most conspicuous ghost of the *Commedia* makes a stand. The almost shockingly strong and unexpected "Ragion" opens the second stanza, and when we know for sure, with that infinitely famous "Donna mi prega" as the final line, that we have been listening to the now-faint voice of Guido Cavalcanti, we smile, remembering that first "Ragion"—we know now it is a sly pun, Petrarch playing, syntactically, with the allusion to a "reason" with which, in veiled and hushed tones, Dante has banished him from literary history altogether. But this beginning of the Cavalcantian stanza is thus also intimately tied to the stanzaic chapter on Arnaut: the echo, the resounding argument is that it is right and just and fitting. Again, too, Petrarch's own most familiar voice(s) melt with, weave in and out of those he is resuscitating: here, Petrarch's lament about the difficulties of beginnings, of writing, of achievement, all melt into the pleas to be heard from the conspicuously silenced Guido of *Inferno* 9. And again, the quarrel over the judgment of history, the history they are writing in their poetries, is with Dante, with Guido but the spoils, the exemplar.

Petrarch's defense of the obliquely but surely damned Guido is as elegant and lyrical as that of Arnaut, single biting jabs, traces of irony: he asks for the chance to please, to caress with his love verses that one with the "occhi santi," and Petrarch's Laura melts momentarily and the one whom Guido is accused of slighting emerges.[9] Guido's miraculously sweet love poetry is heard at a distance; perhaps it is the incomparable "Chi è questa," a lovemaking that, had she been allowed to hear it, would certainly have given those blessed eyes the greatest of delights. The otherwise banal and predictable result, the poet blessed above all others, is now no slap at the hubris of the other's version of the damned and the blessed in literary history. And it is Guido, in Petrarch's pointed revision, who will come out on top ("e me beato sopra gli altri amanti!") because of his great poem of reason, written in truth and for truth and because it was necessary to say, because the lady asked for it, in truth:

"Ma più quand'io dirò senza mentire." Guido did not stray from the right path, Guido did not lie, Guido was on his right path; his Lady asked him to talk about such things.

> Vaghi pensier che così passo passo
> scorto m'avete a ragionar tant'alto:
> vedete che Madonna à 'l cor di smalto
> sì forte ch'io per me dentro nol passo.
> Ella non degna di mirar sì basso
> che di nostre parole
> curi, ché 'l ciel non vole,
> al qual pur contrastando i' son già lasso;
> onde come nel cor m'induro e 'naspro,
> "Così nel mio parlar voglio esser aspro."

Yearning thoughts, which thus step by step have led me to such high speech: you see that my lady has a heart of such hard stone that I cannot by myself pass within it. She does not deign to look so low as to care about our words; for the heavens do not wish it, and resisting them I am already weary; therefore as in my heart I become hard and bitter: "So in my speech I wish to be harsh."

This is the centerpiece, the summit: in the middle of the poem, in the third of the five stanzas, Petrarch reproaches Dante with yet a third ghost, one with which Dante himself deals repeatedly in the *Commedia*, one whose guts are spilled out in the first half of the *Vita nuova*—Dante before his conversion. But this is Petrarch's younger and more vulnerable Dante, a different voice is talking, and it is the same younger Dante we glimpse in Borges's essays on Francesca and on Beatrice, a Dante whose heart will, indeed, turn to stone in the very cold shadows of a love whose greatest mercy and passion is a ghost of a smile. The conceit of the troubadours was wrong, was reversed hyperbole—the single weak smile does not sustain the fainthearted poet and lover. At the apex, then, of Petrarch's counterhistory are Dante's brilliant, sparkling, tough *petrose*, a poetry abandoned by Dante just as Guido and Arnaut were. Once again, the erratic and partial touches, those touchstones of the lyric both revive a past and banish the memory of the canto after canto of sustained arguments, of the well-ordered history of a neat and well-ordered universe: Dante's powerfully lyric voice of the *rime petrose* appears and takes charge, and it tells us that it is this, finally, this bitterness and impenetrability of Madonna, that has created the later, tougher Dante. Petrarch whispers the same dark and scurrilous thought that Borges suggests through the rhetorical ploy of the unsought but fervent denial: that Dante is embittered and envious, and in his hardness the lover turns away from love and damns it. Francesca is an object of envy and vengeance; Borges plants the seed, tries to deny, falls back.

> Infinitamente existió Beatriz para Dante. Dante, muy poco, tal vez nada, para Beatriz; todos nosotros propendemos por piedad, por veneración, a olvidar esta lastimosa discordia inolvidable para Dante.... Pienso en Francesca y en Paolo, unidos para siempre en su Infierno. "Questi, the mai da me non fia diviso...." Con espantoso amor, con ansiedad, con admiratión, con envidia (Borges, *Nueve ensayos*, 152–53)

> For Dante, Beatrice existed forever. But Dante scarcely existed for Beatrice—perhaps not at all. Because we feel sorry for him and because we venerate him, we all try to forget this terrible discrepancy that was unforgettable for Dante.... I recall Paolo and Francesca, together, forever, in their Hell. "This one, who will never be separated from me...." With a frightening love, with anxiety, with admiration, with envy.

> Paolo y Francesca están en el Infierno, él [Dante] se salvara, pero ellos se ban querido y él no ha logrado el amor de la mujer que ama, de Beatriz.... Quienes no comprenden la Comedia dicen que Dante la escribió para vengarse de sus enemigos y premiar a sus amigos. Nada más falso. Nietzsche dijo falsisimamente que Dante es la hiena que versifica entre las tumbas. La hiena que versifica es una contradicción.... (Borges, *Siete noches*, 24–25)

Paolo and Francesca are in Hell, he [Dante] will be saved, but they have loved each other and he has not had the love of the woman he loves, Beatrice.... Those who do not understand the Comedy say that Dante wrote it to take revenge on his enemies and reward his friends. Nothing could be more false. Nietzsche said, ever so falsely, that Dante is the hyena who writes poetry among the tombs. A hyena who writes poetry is a contradiction....

Petrarch's melting of voices with this Dante is confusing, dizzying; in "vaghi pensier" (yearning thoughts) we drift from one poet to the other without boundaries, confused even by "nostre parole" (our words), as if the two were indeed one. But if the *petrose* themselves were as hermetic, many of them, as their title (and clear inspiration in the *trobar clus*) implies, Petrarch once again, as with Arnaut, makes limpid verse appear, opens Dante's heart of stone for him: You see what and how I have come to, you see she is impenetrable (the striking "Madonna a 'l cor di smalto ..." [My lady has a heart of stone ...]), you see that up in the heavens she is too high to look down and grant favor and listen to our poetry ... and I grow weary of this and "in my heart I become hard and bitter" and write hard and bitter verse.... Petrarch attacks the extant version of history head-on: the earlier Dante, he, I, we—for that he is now part of me—loved the crystals of lyric love, but his heart hardened and wearied, he gave up, he couldn't make it, he abandoned the magic of such poetry. And then we hear Borges, his voice now overlapping too, tell the rest of the same story, as he talks about the last encounter with Beatrice:

> Ausente para siempre de Beatriz, solo y quizá humillado, imaginó la escena para imaginar que estaba con ella Desdichadamente para él, felizmente para los siglos que to leerían, la conciencia de que el encounteo era imaginario deformó la visión. De ahí las circunstancias atroces, tanto más infernales, claro está, por ocurrir en el empíreo: la desaparición de Beatriz, el anciano que toma su lugar, su brusca elevación a la Rosa, la fugacidad de la sonrisa y la mirada, el desvío eterno del rostro.... (*Nueve ensayos*, 161)

Separated forever from Beatrice, alone, humiliated perhaps, he imagined the scene to imagine he was with her. Unfortunately for him, and happily for his readers for centuries, his awareness of the fiction of the encounter deformed the vision. From that fact come the atrocious circumstances [of their meeting]—so much more infernal, of course, because it takes place in the empyrean: the disappearance of Beatrice, the old man who takes her place, her rude elevation to the Rose, the fleetingness of the smile and the look, the eternal turning away of her face....

And in the crescendo of different voices, melding voices, that are accumulating in the *canzone*, the hint is that the harshness of the "parlar" is no longer that more or less innocent game of reinventing that earlier lyric tradition, paying homage to predecessors like Arnaut. No, the harshness in this new version of history—and Petrarch shows the cruel ironies and creative possibilities of histories by thus recasting Dante's own verses—is the harshness of his dealings with the Arnauts and the Guidos, the harshness of his unblinking and uncompromising vision of Great and True Poetry.[10]

> Che parlo, o dove sono, et chi m'inganna
> altri chi'io stesso e 'l desiar soverchio?
> Già s'i' trascorro il ciel di cerchio in cerchio
> nessun pianeta a pianger mi condanna;
> se mortal velo il mio veder appana
> che colpa è de le stelle
> o de le cose belle?
> Meco si sta chi dì et notte m'affanna
> poi the del suo piacer mi fe' gir grave
> "La dolce vista e 'l bel guardo soave."

What am I saying? or where am I? and who deceives me but myself and my excessive desire? Nay, if I run through the sky from sphere to sphere, no planet condemns me to weeping. If a mortal veil dulls my sight, what fault is it of the stars or of beautiful things? With me dwells one who night and day troubles me since she made me go heavy with the pleasure of "The sweet sight of her and her lovely soft glance."

Perhaps it is the multiplicity of voices that is confusing. Who knows how many of these poets are saying the same thing, went through the same crises: "What poetry do I write, what punishment exists beyond my own insatiable Desire?" Petrarch speaks here, pointedly, not only for himself, and not even only for the other three whose shadows and echoes pop in and out of this song, but for all poets, for the Poet that struggles with voices, with postures, with ideas. Once again, an almost cruelly simple opening has struck us at heart, given us the terms of engagement: "Che parlo?"—"What am I saying?"

And in the struggle with the response we sense the presence, still, again, of the most important interlocutor, Dante, of course, a Dante now beyond the stark lyric of stony rhymes, a Dante whose bitterness the more innocent voice of Petrarch reproaches: it is not written in the circles of the heavens that one must weep, that one must turn to sights beyond simple beauties. The inherent but often incomprehensible preciousness of the lyric, already captured by Arnaut, sitting in his field singing, reappears here, and certainly nowhere more so than in the starkly simple and sweet couplet "che colpa è delle stelle / o de le cose belle?"

The value of poetry is inherent and in its reflections of other inherent beauties. The poet here is laden down, night and day, with that beauty and that sweetness and simplicity, "the sweet sight of her and her lovely soft glance." Hearing Cino da Pistoia's voice at the end of this stanza, we confirm what we intuited: that the voices resounding here are those that played back and forth in *Purgatorio* 24, that this is Petrarch's visit to and engagement with the *dolce stil nuovo*. Again, Dante is reproached for abandonment of an earlier version of himself, one shared, in poetic moments of far simpler bliss and harmony, with Guido and Lapo and Cino himself. But the reproach is losing its edgy tone, for the voice of Petrarch here is hinting that it is Dante being left behind, running from one sphere to the next.

> Tutte le cose di the 'l mondo è adorno
> uscir buone de man del maestro eterno,
> ma me che così a dentro non discerno

abbaglia il bel che mi si mostra intorno;
et s'al vero splendor giamai ritorno
l'occhio non po star fermo,
così l' à fatto infermo
pur la sua propria colpa, et non quel giorno
ch' i' volsi in ver l'angelica beltade
"Nel dolce tempo de la prima etade."

All things with which the world is beauteous came forth good from the hands of the eternal Workman: but I, who do not discern so far within, am dazzled by the beauty that I see about me, and if I ever return to the true splendor, my eye cannot stay still, it is so weakened by its very own fault, and not by that day when I turned toward her angelic beauty: "In the sweet time of my first age."

All the shadows and ghosts of Dante were, indeed, being left behind, and now, having rehearsed all the arguments, having listened to the voices, learned from the voices of all those poets and poetries, Petrarch emerges triumphant: the lyric poet in the First Age after lyric poetry has been cast aside and condemned and abandoned. Petrarch will prove that history, that judgment, premature—or rather, he will prove the greater power, for history, of the future over the past. He brings us back to himself: the himself of the earliest stage, the "prima etade," first *canzone* of the same work in which this *canzone* is embedded, the *Rime sparse*. But it is more, of course, than the cleverness of the structural arrangement: 23 is a different version of the Poet's coming of age, as might well be surmised by its incipit. The one hundred and sixty-nine verses of the poem—indeed, structurally, the first long poem and thus a pointed hiatus and retrospective (the second of the collection, if one counts as first, as one must, the opening sonnet)—trace and recall, in flashes and suggestions, the genesis of poetry for a Petrarch struggling with and dwelling on just what he is, what he can be: "Lasso, the son? the fui?" (30). Echoes here, throughout this poem, where the struggle is more with Ovidian voices and with what Laura shall be, of 70.

And in 70, in this last stanza of the *canzone*, there is still one last jab at the nemesis who tried to write him, Petrarch, out of poetic history before he had even had a chance to write himself in. "I, who do not discern so far within"—you who imagine you can know the workings, the whys and the reasons of the *maestro eterno*, are clearly deceived. I am simply dazzled by the simple beauty, my eye, my poetry, my soul will write that—and that, of course, is the truest reflection of the eternal "workman," to shine back out into his universe its simplest and most dazzling beauties, in the simple dazzle of their incomprehensibility, in the confusing simplicity of a lyric voice. I am Maker, you are mere Reader.

One is struck that Durling, whose translations hew closely, although never pedantically or unlyrically, to Petrarch's text, chooses to translate *maestro* here as "workman." The translation is justifiable philologically, and the precise context of "uscir buone de man," with a palpable sense of the simple manual labor involved in such creation, adds to the conviction. (And is that Eliot's echo we hear in the background, "Issues from the hand of God, the simple soul ..." his bittersweet reflections on Dante in *Animula*?) Most of all, to summon the "maestro" here is to throw us back, once more and with a vengeance now, to the central cantos of *Purgatorio* where Cino's *dolce stil nuovo* and Arnaut converge and where Dante, finally, laments their limitations. Petrarch too says out loud what the mad and heretic Pound will rant and rave about: God himself is the *fabbro* that Dante has disdained; he makes simple and good things with his hands, he issues them into the world. You cannot disdain me. It is I, that "simple" lyric poet, echoing and repeating His work, His kind of near-blind creation and issue, who am closest to the Maker himself. I run with the wind who speaks Paradise.

IV

Existe ese Aleph en to íntimo de una piedra? Lo he visto cuando vi todas las cosas y to he olvidado? Nuestra mente es porosa para el olvido; yo mismo estoy falseando y perdiendo, bajo la trágica erosión de los años, los rasgos de Beatriz. (Borges, "El Aleph," *El Aleph*)

Does this Aleph exist in the heart of a stone? Did I see it there in the cellar when I saw all things, and have I now forgotten it? Our minds are porous and forgetfulness seeps in; I myself am distorting and losing, under the wearing away of the years, the face of Beatriz.

The name of Beatrice is the last on Borges's lips in "The Aleph," the vanishing Beatriz fading away, inevitably, with time, treacherous and false time that erodes what once seemed clear and crystalline and unforgettable. We are astonishingly close to a Petrarchan poetics here, and this rude and sad ending throws us back to the beginning of the story, of course, for we are forced to realize that the entire narration, which hardly seemed so at first, was from that final perspective of sand escaping inexorably through the fingers—and created, no less obviously, in the bittersweet, half-successful, half-failed effort to retrieve, to halt and turn back that erosion. So we return, as we must, to the beginning, to the opening sentence of "The Aleph"—and the signs are all there, embarrassingly obvious now:

> La candente mañana de febrero en que Beatriz Viterbo murió, después de una imperiosa agonía que no se rebajó un solo instante ni al sentimentalismo ni al miedo, noté que las carteleras de fierro de la Plaza Constitución habían renovado no se qué aviso de cigarrillos rubios; el hecho me dolió, pues comprendí que el incesante y vasto universo ya se apartaba de ella y que ese cambio era el primero de una serie infinita.

> On the burning February morning Beatriz Viterbo died, after braving an agony that never for a single moment gave way to self-pity or fear, I noticed that the sidewalk billboards around Constitution Plaza were advertising some new brand or other of American cigarettes. The fact pained me, for I realized that the wide and ceaseless universe was already slipping away from her and that this slight change was the first in an endless series.

Death and memory and the apparent vanity of doing much about either: death comes and memory, just as inexorably, slips away—except, of course (although this we cannot, we need not, be told too directly), through the magical powers of poetry, of writing. Borges has tricked us, with too-obvious names and story lines, into thinking we are in Dante's universe; but we are, far more so, in Petrarch's universe, that universe of belief in the great and powerful magic of poetry—that lyricism that alone can stand up to the erosions of time and deaths and changing universes. The story's second sentence, following hard on that "this slight change was the first in an endless series," begins, "Cambiará el universo, pero yo no, pensé con melancólica vanidad ..." (The universe may change but not me, I thought with a certain sad vanity ...). Few phrases could have summoned Petrarch as poignantly and empathetically as that *melancólica vanidad*: the last stanza of that remarkable opening sonnet reverberates vividly—"et del mio vaneggiar vergogna è 'l frutto ..." (and of my raving, shame is the fruit ...).

The Poet, Borges like Petrarch before him, sits in melancholy contemplation of that wasteland of memory and of the follies of youth, but he, they, are no less struck with the new life that has come from those ruins, the vital poetry, the song, the story, that, in an unsayably different way captures—or does it really create?—both ruin and a fleetingly glorious past. While a Virgil or a Dante or an Eliot might see in such a wasteland the destruction from which a new empire or greater, wholer Truth is waiting to be crafted, these poets harbor an ambition both more and less astonishing: to play back, to reinvent, the magic and the beauties of imperfections, dispersals. The loss is irretrievable but a new magic is brought forth. The *rime* are *sparse*, scattered, because that is the shape of the universe and the human condition. The lyric form—and Borges's short stories, particularly in that necessary context of the omnivorous and overweening novel, are as strikingly lyrical as the Petrarchan sonnet—refracts that liminality and ambiguity back at both poet and audience and revels in their bittersweet beauty. Such language both cannot really say what can be said directly and says far more than that.[11] And this, of course, is the heart of their opposition to Dante's logology.[12] The second sentence continues: "Alguna vez, to sé, mi vana devoción la había exasperado; muerta, yo podía consagrarme a su memoria, sin esperanza, pero también sin humiliación" (I knew that at times my fruitless devotion had annoyed her; now that she was dead I could devote myself to her memory, without hope, but also without humiliation). Voices come and go, poets fade in and out; the Dante that is being constructed here is that same one we find venerated, but frankly pitied, in the Borgesian essays, humiliated by a hard and unrelenting Beatrice, a lover whose heart has turned to stone, whose poetry turned beyond love. Even in death, in the invention of literature, that is, there is no hope: Dante will not be happy with crumbs, with imperfection.

The multiple voices of "The Aleph" continue to tell this story of a Petrarchan Dante, a story told in the first person by an Argentinian who calls himself Borges. The Borges liberated from humiliation by the death of Beatriz celebrates her birthday, the thirtieth of April, every year after her death with a visit to her house, a house lived in by her father (a very fleeting presence) and a first cousin with a name overwrought with meanings, Carlos Argentino Daneri.[13] Borges comes to look at her pictures. The birthday visits become pilgrimages, anniversaries, for years, then decades during which, through accident as well as calculation on Borges's part, the visits have become more intimate and Borges gets to know the peculiar Daneri, fatuous, pompous, useless. "Su actividad mental es continua, apasionada, versátil y del todo insignificante" (His mental activity was continuous, deeply felt, far-ranging, and—all in all—meaningless). It turns out, finally, that he is a writer of literature:

> Tan ineptas me parecieron esas ideas [Daneri had just held forth on how modern man had made himself complete, autonomous] tan pomposa y tan vasta su exposición, que las relacioné inmediatamente con la literatura; le dije que por qué no las escribía. Previsiblemente respondió que ya to había hecho....
>
> So foolish did his ideas seem to me, so pompous and so drawn out his exposition, that I linked them at once to literature and asked him why he didn't write them down. As might be foreseen, he answered that he had already done so....

For years, in fact, Daneri has been writing a work that will express a total vision of the universe that comprehends all previous authors, all matters; he is writing the globe itself in verse, inch by inch. Borges becomes Daneri's listener, reader—no longer merely the yearly visitor on the occasion of Beatrice's birthday. Borges humors him—and he is again referred to as "el primo hermano aquel de Beatriz"—clearly because it is a tie to her, it allows him to say her name. But then, as an open manifestation of how inexorably time and change runs over so many things, Daneri's ancestral home, which for Borges is the last material tie to Beatriz, is threatened with demolition. Because of the tie to the dead woman, Borges is more than alarmed, but Daneri is virtually hysterical, because, he confesses, he needs the house in order to finish his book, his poem of the universe, "pues en un ángulo del sótano había un Aleph. Aclaró que un Aleph es uno de los puntos del espacio que contienen todos los puntos" (because down in the cellar there was an Aleph. He explained that an Aleph is one of the points in space that contains all other points). The rest of the story spins out in a tone that fluctuates between the comic-ironic (hilarious and absurd conversations between Daneri and Borges, Borges deciding in one instant that Daneri is mad, that for that matter Beatriz was as well, and then snatching a moment alone in the living room to talk to her portrait) and a cutting seriousness. One scarcely knows whether Borges is smiling or not as he goes down the cellar stairs: Daneri allows Borges himself to descend to see the precious Aleph, and it turns out it does exist, after all, and it does contain the universe. It is Borges, then, at that moment, who is faced head-on with the great problem Daneri has already tackled, and whose inadequacy at the task was condescendingly disdained—how to describe that whole, universal vision: "Arribo, ahora, el inefable centro de mi relato; empieza, aquí, mi desesperación de escritor.... Cómo transmitir a los otros el infinito Aleph, que mi temerosa memoria apenas abarca? ... Por to demás, el problem central es irresoluble: la enumeración, siquiera parcial, de unconjunto infinito" (I arrive now at the ineffable core of my story. And here begins my despair as a writer.... How, then, can I translate into words the limitless Aleph, which my floundering mind can scarcely encompass? ... Really, what I want to do is impossible, for any listing of an endless series is doomed to be infinitesimal). Borges is stuck, and yet he does decide to try it, and gives an obviously partial and scattered list of events, places, and all manner of things, the two pages or so are, finally, high lyric, poetry far removed from the presumptuous narrative with the difficult form Daneri had adopted. And while Daneri and his epic poem seem never to flinch at the possibility of recounting and making diachronic a vision that has no time, Borges's lyric is rooted in its own insufficiencies and ends.

> Vi la reliquia atroz de lo que deliciosamente había sido Beatriz Viterbo, vi la circulación de mi oscura sangre, vi el engranaje del amor y la modificación de la muerte, vi el

Aleph, desde todos los puntos, vi en el Aleph la tierra, y en la tierra otra vez el Aleph y en el Aleph la tierra, vi mi cara y mis vísceras, vi tu cara, y sentí vértigo y lloré, *porque mis ojos habían visto ese objeto secreto y conjetural, cuyo nombre usurpan los hombres, pero que ningún hombre ha mirado: el inconcebible universo.*
Sentí infinita veneración, infinita lástima.

I saw the rotted dust and bones that had once deliciously been Beatriz Viterbo; I saw the circulation of my own dark blood; I saw the coupling of love and the modification of death; I saw the Aleph from every point and angle, and in the Aleph I saw the earth and in the earth the Aleph and in the Aleph the earth; I save my own face and my own bowels; I saw your face; and I felt dizzy and wept, *for my eyes had seen that secret and conjectured object whose name is common to all men but which no man has looked upon—the unimaginable universe.*
I felt infinite wonder, infinite pity.

But Borges and even the ridiculous Daneri *have* seen the "inconceivable universe"—and Borges, the author now, rather than the narrator, has succeeded once again in mystifying us, in giving us a tone, above all, that is at once derisive and admiring, credulous and incredulous. This is that same Borges, indeed, who writes about Dante Alighieri with both veneration and pity, who tells us on every page of his Dante criticism that what Dante did could scarcely be done and is thus the greatest literary achievement ever; but one never gets away from that tone of pity, that hint that that is all, somehow, something other than poetry. The most coherent and comprehensive recent study of Borges and Dante, focusing on the Aleph, concludes, roughly, that this is far from a somewhat simple Dante parody (the conventional line of criticism) but rather an assertion of the importance of a method of significant omission for the modern poetics of total vision, as opposed to the encyclopaedic or epic method of total enumeration (Thiem:108).

But Thiem believes that Borges's (positive) model really *is* Dante, particularly the *Paradiso*, and thus falls into the critical trap that author—predecessors are either venerated or not—or that the options here are either veneration or parody. But Borges himself gave the most direct statement: *I felt infinite veneration and infinite pity*. Close readings of Borges's direct readings of Dante, of the *Paradiso* particularly, reveal ample quantities of that same paradox, which is perhaps more closely linked to the much-abused Petrarchan oxymoron than one might have thought. And Borges, the narrator now, closes the book on the Aleph after that conspicuously brief prose-poem about it: he refuses to discuss it with Daneri, he leaves the house forever, the house is demolished, he starts to forget it.... The Aleph, in his poetics, becomes nothing more and nothing less than other experiences and memory traces, imperfectly crystallized in a poem. It is only Daneri who believes it is writable, who finishes his book and wins a prize for it. The story itself ends, as we have already seen, with that throwback to its beginning, that infinitely moving and surprising statement that he is beginning to forget even Beatriz.

Borges's Beatriz, especially in conjunction with his essays on Beatrice in the *Purgatorio* and *Paradiso*, is a fulcrum of images and meanings, the stark emblem of why pity and sadness and disappointments haunt all those pages; and it is through her that we sense most clearly those great misgivings Borges has about Dante. For the pity exists not because she is dead but because the author never knew how to recover her, even in death, and because her cruelty, her absences, finally made him turn away. It should be clear from the necessarily fragmented recounting of "The Aleph" I have given that there is a cacophony of poetic voices in the story—and that they are attached to more than one character: the Dante created here is as much the Borges as the Daneri. (In great measure, of course, this is what prevents its being a simple parody.) For Dante as Daneri, Beatriz is a necessary but unspoken attachment, a cousin whose pictures are still scattered throughout his house, and he is a man who welcomes a stranger to his house to commemorate her birthday, years after her death. But her name never passes his lips—it is never even clear he understood what that Borges was doing in his house every thirtieth of April—and it is eventually evident that his great attachment is, of course, the Aleph, his inspiration, his source, his magic touchstone.

At first Daneri himself has no importance for Borges except as the cousin to the dead Beatriz—a Beatriz, one is compelled to note, who is never described as alive except at the instant Borges comes to the conclusion that Daneri is mad, and decides that she probably was as well.

> Beatriz (yo mismo suelo repetirlo) era una mujer, una niña, de una clarividencia casi implacable, pero había en ella negligencias, distracciones, desdenes, verdaderas crueldades, que tal vez reclamaban una explicacián patológica.
>
> Beatriz (I myself often say it) was a woman, a child, with almost uncanny powers of clairvoyance, but forgetfulness, distractions, contempt, and a streak of cruelty were also in her, and perhaps these called for a pathological explanation.

The beloved, then, was infinitely unworthy, that same Beatrice who is created cruel even in the *Purgatorio* and *Paradiso*. And then, slowly, Daneri becomes much more, and Borges's remaining attachments to her are merely incantational, like the habit of a prayer, and a vulgar one at that. Daneri, finally, is the link not to his cousin but to the Aleph itself, and thus, for Borges, Beatriz herself is but the first step to the grand vision, to that moment of clairvoyance and ineffability in the basement of her ancestral home. This, in the end, was all she really gave him, although it would seem it was perhaps a great deal, because she appears to have been otherwise unable to be fulfilling at all. Borges, like Petrarch, is a stunning and magical historian and in a handful of lines can lay bare the ambition and the hurt—each in their own way part of the obsession with truth—that are two sides of the same coin:

> Carlos Argentino observó, con admiración rencorosa, que no creía errar en el epiteto al calificar de sólido el prestigio logrado en todos los círculos por Alvaro Melían Lafinur, hombre de letras ... yo tenía que hacerme portavoz de dos méritos inconclusos: la perfección formal y el rigor científico, "porque ese dilatado jardín de tropos, de figuras, de galanuras, no tolera un solo detalle que no confirme la severa verdad." Agregó que Beatriz siempre se había distraído con Alvaro.
>
> Carlos Argentino [Daneri] remarked, with admiration and envy, that surely he could not be far wrong in qualifying with the epithet "solid" the prestige enjoyed in every circle by

Alvaro Melían Lafinur, a man of letters ... he [Daneri] suggested I make myself spokesman for two of the book's undeniable virtues—formal perfection and scientific rigor— "inasmuch as this wide garden of metaphors, of figures of speech, of elegances, is inhospitable to the least detail not strictly upholding of truth." He added that Beatriz had always been taken with Alvaro.[14]

Hurt and ambition. Little wonder, given such a reading of the *Vita nuova* and the *Commedia*, that Borges prefaces his remarks to the encounter with Beatrice in the *Paradiso* with that arresting "I want to comment on the most moving [literally, full of pathos] verses literature has ever produced." But there is more than even that, implicitly, that is pathetic, pitiable, for Borges the writer and the consumer and inventor of writers is not so irreducibly romantic that even the most irremediable of romantic attachments would in and of itself provoke such great pathos in him. Clearly, it is the result, at least in this case, as he sees it, of that failure in love: the abandonment of even the possibility of love poetry for the Aleph in the basement, for that clairvoyance, that universal and epic vision. For the sight of what others might call empire, or grandeur, or God.

> Se Virgilio et Omero avessin visto
> quel sole il qual vegg'io con gli occhi miei,
> tutte lor forze in dar fama a costei
> avrian posto et l'un stil coll'altro misto,
>
> di che sarebbe Enea turbato, et tristo
> Achille, Ulisse et gli altri semidei,
> et quel the resse anni cinquantasei
> si bene il mondo, et quel ch'ancise Egisto....

If Virgil and Homer had seen that sun which I see with my eyes, they would have exerted all their powers to give her fame and would have mixed together the two styles:

For which Aeneas would be angry; and Achilles, Ulysses, and the other demigods, and he who ruled the world so well for fifty-six years, and he whom Aegisthus killed, would all be sad.... (Petrarch, *Rime sparse*, Poem 186, first two stanzas of sonnet)

V

THE ALEPH

What eternity is to time, the Aleph is to space. In eternity, all time—past, present, and future—coexists simultaneously. In the Aleph, the sum total of the spatial universe is to be found in a tiny shining sphere barely over an inch across. When I wrote my story, I recalled Wells's dictum that in a tale of the fantastic, if the story is to be acceptable to the mind of the reader, only one fantastic element should be allowed at a time. For example, though Wells wrote a book about the invasion of Earth by Martians, and another book about a single invisible man in England, he was far too wise to attempt a novel about an invasion of our planet by an army of invisible men. Thinking of the Aleph as a thing of wonder, I placed it in as drab a setting as I could imagine—a small cellar in a nondescript house in an unfashionable quarter of Buenos Aires. In the world of the *Arabian Nights*, such things as magic lamps and rings are left lying about and nobody cares; in our skeptical world, we have to tidy up any alarming or out-of-the-way element. Thus, at the end of "The Aleph," the house has to be pulled down and the shining sphere destroyed with it.

Once, in Madrid, a journalist asked me whether Buenos Aires actually possessed an Aleph. I nearly yielded to temptation and said yes, but a friend broke in and pointed out that were such an object to exist it would not only be the most famous thing in the world but would renew our whole conception of time, astronomy, mathematics, and space. "Ah," said the journalist, "so the entire thing is your invention. I thought it was true because you gave the name of the street." I did not dare tell him that the naming of streets is not much of a feat.

My chief problem in writing the story lay in what Walt

> Whitman had very successfully achieved—the setting down of a limited catalog of endless things. The task, as is evident, is impossible, for such chaotic enumeration can only be simulated, and every apparently haphazard element has to be linked to its neighbor either by secret association or by contrast.
>
> "The Aleph" has been praised by readers for its variety of elements: the fantastic, the satiric, the autobiographical, and the pathetic. I wonder whether our modern worship of complexity is not wrong, however. I wonder whether a short story should be so ambitious. Critics, going even further, have detected Beatrice Portinari in Beatriz Viterbo, Dante in Daneri, and the descent into hell in the descent into the cellar. I am, of course, duly grateful for these unlooked-for gifts.
>
> Beatriz Viterbo really existed and I was very much and hopelessly in love with her. I wrote my story after her death. Carlos Argentino Daneri is a friend of mine, still living, who to this day has never suspected he is in the story. The verses are a parody of his verse. Daneri's speech on the other hand is not an exaggeration but a fair rendering. The Argentine Academy of Letters is the habitat of such specimens. (Borges, "Commentaries," in *The Aleph and Other Stories*, 263–64)

It is one of the most recent and generally felicitous commonplaces of Petrarch criticism that Petrarch's struggles with defining himself and his poetry are at the very heart of the *Rime sparse*. It is also understood now that Petrarch's disavowal of Dante, both direct and through conspicuous silences, is itself to be dismissed, for Dante's presence is, finally, as conspicuous (if not more so) in Petrarch's vernacular poetry as that of any other of his poetic ancestors, those he chooses not to deny. But it is far less well understood how closely these two issues are interwoven; and a critical tradition that once accepted the Dante exclusion, as it did the literal truths of a Laura and her anniversaries, now largely feels it is sufficient to merely note the conspicuous falsehood of the denial of Dante while it acknowledges his many presences in the *Rime sparse*. Such denial is assumed to be either a normal thing to do and thus not worth dwelling on—or perhaps it is that the implications are far too banal, shallow, and embarrassing to be worth much space and time, particularly since we now know it to be a false denial and it no longer prevents us from finally seeing the Dante allusions, calques, "influence."

But I would argue that in fact the particular textual uses Petrarch makes of Dante are colored and shaped by that search for definitions of self and poetry, and that a necessary part of that search is bound up with the most difficult of ancestral relations for him, that with Dante. In other words, given the critical context that Petrarch at one level overtly and unambiguously absents Dante from the *Rime sparse*, it seems problematic to deal with the presences one then does detect—the structural affinity, the verbal echo, the allusion—as if that denial simply had not been uttered, or were a slip of some sort caused by an unrelated and simple personal jealousy or some other flaw that was somehow irrelevant to the poetry itself. We are hardly dealing with banal or pseudo-psychological analysis here, but rather with a remarkably powerful and meaningful juxtaposition that is potentially of central importance to at least one possible reading of the *Rime sparse*.

It is instructive to note that Borges scholars have been puzzled by the fact that Borges plays Petrarch in this way as well: he does not, first of all, actually name Dante in "El Aleph," a story which includes direct acknowledgements of a number of other authors. Most of all, the "history" of this little story has been largely written by Borges himself—once again in a stunning lyricism, in that commentary on "The Aleph" that speaks powerfully on the issue of literary history and its makings. In the middle of this combination of explicit self-analysis and Borgesized literary criticism, he says it right there in black and white, in a sharp evocation of the positivism and linearity of the dominant critical mode, for all to see: my story is a simple thing, not ambitious, and to see Beatrice in Beatriz and Dante in Daneri is part of the obsessive historicizing of literary critics. Not only that: the truth is there really was a Beatriz Viterbo and I really did adore her and there really was a Daneri and he really is my friend....

The numerous interpretations of this curiosity are not unlike those in the equally curious case of Petrarch: one notes it and goes on, or calls it an instance of "Bloomian anxiety" and goes on, no less blithely, as if the problem of a complex relationship has been dealt with by the simple incantation of Bloom. Again, the fundamental critical problem that emerges is that overt references in a context in which the very possibility of such references being made has been excluded are very specially marked. And in both cases, one must begin with the most innocent of observations, namely that the denials of "influence" from Dante are transparently—intentionally—false and ludicrous, *first and foremost to their authors*. Certainly one cannot read Borges's paragraph denying Dante's presence with any less of a smile than the paragraph where he tells us about the "journalist"—another species of critic, no doubt—who asks whether there really is an Aleph ... and who believed it had to be all "true" or all "false." Again, the issue is settled in the last paragraph, after the denial of Dante's Beatrice and the assertion of the true love of his own Beatriz: Borges the Maker is showing us he can play any game, including the I-write-the-Truth game. Meanwhile, no less importantly, in the denial of the undeniable, what is also taking place is the establishment of a parallel universe. For both Borges and Petrarch, Dante is explicitly made what he was and is, historically and personally to one, canonically for the other, as for ourselves: the very parameters of a universe, a fundamental guideline so obviously present that it is precisely the strong interpretations within the text, those transformations and remarkable interpretations, that constitute the real rejection. It is not the silence or the denial in Petrarch or Borges that excludes Dante; quite the contrary: the very conspicuousness of the gesture is what asserts the inevitability of Dante's presence. And, concomitantly and conversely, it is within such an inevitable presence, it is the citations, the game of reenactment, that are used to deny; for denial means a tampering with the future for poets of this magnitude, it means that brand of historical revision that powerfully recasts and rewrites a predecessor.

And at the very beginning is the denial of that diachronic concept of history, a concept that is strongly bound to the epic, to the Daneris, to the literary historians who see "influence" in such positivistic ways. Such linearity is inimical to the "simpler" project at hand, to the synchronic moment of lyricism that shuffles time around and rearranges it, that tells us that metaphysics is that simple and atemporal list of the universe. "What eternity is to time, the Aleph is to space. In eternity, all time—past, present, and future—coexist simultaneously." The irony, then, lies simply in the fact that although the Aleph does exist, it vanishes the instant we try and tell it rather than suggest it. This is a step not so very different from Dante's own faint praise; this is veneration and pity, a reverence that distances, or perhaps that recognizes and emphasizes the great distances that are already there. The irony, if irony there can be in what is at least in part a natural cycle, is that Dante is left behind in the historiography created by the later lyricists precisely because he turns away, in their visions (and to a great extent in his own as we see in his treatment of Arnaut), from simple love song to universal poet. Here, in this telling of it, Dante's heart did turn to stone, and he lost his youthful ability to transform love, an inherently inadequate and transitory phenomenon, into a poetry of perpetual desire: his Beatrice was never alive enough, powerful enough—like Virgil and Homer, he did not have a sun resplendent enough. And both writer-historians, Borges and Petrarch, understand intimately—and with this the subject of their analysis would scarcely disagree—that at the heart of Dante's conversion is that same issue of the nature of poetry and what it can and should do and be. Not, Does the Aleph exist, does Beatrice exist—only those who cannot conceive literature at all would ask such a question—but, How and where do they exist: have I made them or have I revealed them?

In their recreation of Dante, both Borges and Petrarch are, of course, exercising the same powerful prerogative of shaping and fashioning an ancestry that Dante himself used incomparably, and that most if not all writers do to some extent, as Borges himself has pointed out. Once again, time is of the essence and literary history is a great deal like the Aleph, "a tiny shining sphere barely over an inch across." In fact, if we go back to the beginning once again, we understand the frankly subversive historical project that is "The Aleph." The story begins with two epigraphs, in English and from a purposefully scattered past, a past that sheds light on the future. From *Hamlet*: "O God! I could be bounded in a nutshell, and count myself a King of infinite space"; and from *Leviathan*: "But they will teach us that Eternity is the Standing still of the Present Time, a *Nunc-stans* (as the Schools call it); which neither they, nor any else understand, no more than they would a *Hic-stans* for an infinite greatness of Place." And while Dante casts the whole enterprise in absolute moral terms that seek to fix future time in its grasp, the kabbalists and magicians who follow in his wake will mock that reading of time; only the young and foolish think one can master time and be the King of infinite space. Crucially, these are the poets of a different kind of Belief, and they insist on a different kind of moral hierarchy: they believe in what is sayable, in the superb *voice* that tells us about how much he really loved Beatriz. In these terms, one finds it easier to understand the curious structure of the *Rime sparse*, in which the opening sonnet appears to undercut the love poetry that will follow, but at closer inspection in fact denies the "conversion" that will supposedly take place.[15] In these terms both Borges and Daneri in "The Aleph" are highly privileged—but probably unique. Both Petrarch and Borges look Vision, and the possibilities of writing transcendent Truths, in the face and turn away—perhaps, finally, because it could only be done by Dante, it had been done by Dante and thus could not possibly be redone. Perhaps because they thought it other, far inferior to, the magic lyricism of which they were both masters and fervent believers. There is the reverence and veneration, there, in the silences of denials, the most charming and sincere of acknowledgements: Dante was and is the unique visionary and universal and inimitable Poet. Of course, now we see that it is not Dante we should see in Daneri, for Dante is the Aleph itself. And he cannot be retold without grotesque parody.[16]

But it is precisely in the inimitability of his now sacred text, in its wake, that any sort of literary history can follow, and that, of course, is the center of Petrarch's struggle with his notions of self and of his art, a struggle that was as voracious, and ultimately as successful, as it was precisely for the reason that it took place because of Dante and with Dante and against Dante. One can only begin to imagine the extraordinary and oppressive power, personal and literary (and for Petrarch this distinction would have been minor, if it existed at all), of living and working in the close-cropped shadow of Dante's *Commedia*, of Dante's recognition, of the suspicion that the text had now been written, that the love lyric was dead, that any budding poets after him may as well lay down and die—all suspicions inscribed by Dante himself within the *Commedia* and easily decipherable by as formidable a reader as Petrarch.[17] We can hear in the background the noise of fame, treacherous fame, and even more treacherous popularity, both bones of contention, thorns intricately bound up with the omnipotent one of language, the *volgare*. Dante has taken more than his fair share; and even in Borges's universe, the flaw of Daneri the writer of the Aleph is that of a kind of voraciousness, that belief that language can be so infinitely expanded and recalibrated and manipulated that it will be able to say the Aleph.

Petrarch grappled painfully, at times ironically, with what the *volgare*, the vernacular, was, and whether he could possibly be a poet of a language that would then be taken over by those, the *volgo*, who had been given access to it—and Dante's own fame and success could in some ways be sneered at because it had slipped away from him, it had been appropriated by an infinitely unworthy public.[18] Petrarch would even come to claim, in the all-revealing letter to Boccaccio, that he had given up "his [Dante's] style of composition to which I devoted myself as a young man, for I feared for my writings ..."—feared that his poetry too would come to be changed as a vernacular language itself is, sung and resung until it was something else altogether, eroded and altered by time itself.[19] The difficulty in interpreting these comments of Petrarch's—and our assumption that he was being hypocritical (or worse, since we know he was very far from abandoning poetry in the vernacular)—is due to two kinds of interference: First, our own knowledge of the history that would follow, i.e., that Petrarch's vernacular poetry would become so substantial and integral a part of the subsequent poetic tradition. Second, our assumption that to say "the vernacular" is to have said one thing, that all styles within the vernacular, in other words, are like each other. But Petrarch was in fact making the crucial distinction between two possible vernacular styles exemplified in crystalline fashion in "The Aleph": the infinite, expansive, and universal style that Daneri tries, a Daneri who in his own muddled way believes that his writing must mirror, must tell and narrate, the infinite Truths of the Aleph; and the elliptical and allusive style, radically incomplete, that is what Borges, the narrator, comes up with, scarcely more than a suggestion—that incandescent suggestion that the sparkle is more powerful than the Vision.

Or, perhaps, it is that the gloss is more powerful, more magically subversive, than the master text. For perhaps part of what is taking place here, and what so intimately links together Petrarch and Borges, is the kind of marginality, or looming, potential marginality, with which both are burdened by Dante. In the case of Borges, the argument has been marvelously made by González Echevarría that Borges's Derridian affinities—that starkly kabbalistic attribution of primacy to writing and texts themselves—is rooted in the Latin American writer's inherently marginal position vis-à-vis the European tradition: "The relationship may be understood in the sense suggested by Derrida's epigraphs, as a supplement that repeats the original tradition, by taking its place, by rewriting it from within, but always as if it were from without"

(González Echevarría [1983] 1986b:231). In the end, this is a remarkably precise meditation on what Borges is doing with the Divine Comedy, venerated but hegemonistic, in his "Aleph"—and, in quite different but congruent historical circumstances, what Petrarch and his *Rime sparse* are doing. While in the distant twentieth century Borges would have to create the space for an absence of Dante achieved by the overwhelming and almost caricatured references (to the point of it all seeming to many to be a parody), that overwhelming and probably also caricatured presence was, no doubt, an oppressive reality for Petrarch, a Petrarch whose kindred souls in a number of ways may turn out to be the Latin American writers who have always shared with him that need to work from a "strategic marginality," as González Echevarría has put it.[20]

Thus the genius of Petrarch's defense—self-defense may be more like it—was to use that universality of presence for his own purposes, to write a *Rime sparse* that not only is a parallel universe but a text and a poetry that distinguish themselves clearly, in the apparently silent interstices, from that text that is the bearer of a shockingly powerful new tradition. Petrarch must strike back at the challenge to the future, for the threat of Dante is precisely that, a threat to drown out his voice before it was even raised. Poor Petrarch, a Latin Americanist might be tempted to say. So far from God, so close to Dante. But the Petrarchan voice that emerges under such conditions is one that revels in its powerful fragmentariness and succeeds precisely through proclaiming the superiority of that momentary, perhaps vanishing, but certainly magical glimmer that has characterized other writers who have seen the power inherent in a "commentator's" role, writers like Garcilaso the Inca and Carpentier—and of course Borges. And coyly, craftily, Petrarch will craft for himself the kind of subversive centrality that Dante has, in the end, denied himself: imitability. For, we should notice now all the more clearly, Petrarch's lament about Dante was not that he was imitated (of course not—how could Petrarch, the classicist, lament any such fate?)[21] but rather that he was mistreated by "the rabble," who "mispronounce and mangle his verses." That is the problem with becoming an Aleph: only the Daneris—perhaps from time to time a pitiful Pellico—will be a part of your tradition. To hear Borges tell it, Dante made himself inimitable, and left only to the unwise and untalented the vain hope of a mangled and pompous copying. But there can be no greater fame than the kind of utter imitability inspired by the finely hewn and starkly limited *Canzoniere*.

By going outside (and, we will grant, he says, beyond) the normal human condition, the normal boundaries of writing, Dante made himself unique, the *Commedia* a sacred text; but what he garnered for both in literary history was, inevitably, a place in certain key ways also outside and beyond and above. Petrarch's place, in part because the *Rime sparse* is set up in deliberate and inescapable counterpoint and revision, is paradoxically back within that history, at its center, as a new beginning that is the opposite of the dead end Dante saw as a new life. Petrarch becomes the most vitally imitated poet in the history of poetry. The *Commedia* may not exactly sit on the shelves gathering dust, but like most sacred texts, it is read primarily by the devout and the already converted. More importantly, the *Commedia*, in its inimitable vastness and astonishing ambition, may serve as an absolutely necessary part of one's literary education—as Pound says, "Anyone who don't know the *Commedia* is thereby ignoramus"—but it cannot, as a whole, be held long enough to be the kind of "influential" text that will generate bona fide children rather than fragmented commentary. The failed attempts at following such an overweening model run the gamut from Pellico's *Prigioni* to Pound's *Cantos*. As Freccero notes: "While almost all modern poets can trace the Dantesque ancestry of some of their verses, none can claim him as a model. To speak of Dante's influence, then, is to speak of the ways in which fragments of a no longer vital tradition have been used, often ironically, in order to shape totally different individual talents" (Freccero 1986b:3).[22] Borges tells us, in fact, that the Aleph cannot be rewritten successfully, that it can only convert away from literature, that the Truth project is far too inimical to the literary one. Some days Dante is the Aleph and others he is Daneri.

But how different from Daneri's or Pound's is Petrarch's fate, how different the fame he achieved for himself. Although his name is far less known and his text's name virtually unknown (except among the cognoscenti), his love poetry has reverberated, often quite precisely, in virtually every poet in his wake, with the great love one has of what is imitable. Eschewing a universal *volgare*, he has in most ways escaped the rabble: they do not mispronounce his name or mangle his text, as indeed they do Dante's. But, in a different order altogether, the many different features of the *Rime sparse* are the perpetual and inescapable conceits of the lyric, its rhythms and its fragmented sparkles, the magic incantation whose exact origins are lost in time; and time is irrelevant now. Most of all, there is infinite imitability, even when it is unconscious, in the uncertainties and ambiguities and belief in unknowable and inexpressible magic that are in the Poet Petrarch constructed. Thus, even in the late twentieth century, when lyric has become rock (not, clearly, the *petrose* of Dante), Petrarch's presence is heard and seen everywhere by those who know—even, of course, among those who are consciously oblivious of his existence, or of who the "real" Laura might be, the one constructed in the *Rime sparse*.[23] She has been so vastly influential, we do not even remember her name anymore. We don't need to.

At the end, I return to that vision that Borges has of Dante's pathetic last look at Beatrice, and to Borges's sense of sadness that, as a love story, it had to end that way. In his *Essay* Borges does not quite say—whether by choice or inability is neither clear nor determinable—what "The Aleph" ever so clearly reveals: that such a sad end is (from the point of view of poets like him and like Petrarch, those who have not abandoned a belief in their own powers, their almost limitless shamanism) the just deserts of a poet like Dante who has cast his lot with Truth. That Beatrice, like the Beatriz in Borges's story, can never be anything more than what she was in life; she is trapped in dusty photographs of specific days and accountable hours, chained to realities that were often not so beautiful. How much better, how much simpler, how much more human and poetic, to yield to the temptations of duplicity, to believe in language, to incant and create a lover, to understand that if I say, "Beatriz Viterbo really existed and I was very much and hopelessly in love with her," it is a truth no one can ever deny, and to recognize that "the poet is of the devil's party," as de Man put it. Pellico's great failure in prison comes back to haunt: he yields to virtue and rejects the good story—and then we remember that in so doing he was executing an excellent reading of Dante, a Dante for whom Francesca could be a spectacularly good story, but not, finally, Beatrice. Love should not be blind, just the poet; for in blindness creation may thrive, whereas vision, finally, yields but Truth. And there is poor Dante, he tells us, vast, great, inimitable achievement in hand, such a gift as no man has ever made for a woman; and he has come such a long way, constructed such a monumental edifice, all to get to her again, to try once again. But the Truth is still, of course, the same: she turns her back, she walks away.

Notes

1. Borges wrote widely and in a number of different genres about Dante, but his overtly critical views seem to find fairly definitive expression in the collection of nine essays entitled *Nueve ensayos dantescos* (Borges 1982). I have also used the single essay entitled "La divina comedia" included in the collection *Siete noches* (Borges 1980), which almost without exception includes the same views and focuses on the same cantos and the same cast of characters (Francesca, Ugolino, Ulysses, Beatrice), except that the nine essays range somewhat more widely and less predictably. Translations of citations from both these critical texts are my own. Finally, although Borges's allusions to Dante in his fiction are also numerous and very widely spread—see Thiem 1988 for a comprehensive recent compilation—I have focused primarily on the most direct and most famous of Borges's stories "about" Dante, "The Aleph," first published in 1945; the cited translation is by di Giovanni, in collaboration with the author (Borges 1970).

2. The logology as a reflection of the universe and all its truths is explicitly recognized by Borges at the outset of his *Nueve ensayos*: "Imaginemos, en una biblioteca oriental, una lámina pintada hace muchos siglos.... Declina el día, se fatiga la luz y a medida que nos internamos en el grabado, comprendemos que no hay cosa en la tierra que no esté ahí. Lo que fue, lo que es y to que será, la historia del pasado y la del futuro, las cosas que he tenido y las que tendré, todo ello nos espera en algún lugar de ese laberinto tranquilo.... He fantaseado una obra mágica, una lámina que también fuera un microcosmo; el poema de Dante es esa lámina de ámbito universal" (85) (Let us imagine, in an oriental library, an illustration painted centuries ago.... Day is done, the light dims and as we become a part of the engraving we realize that there is nothing on earth that is not there. What was, what is, what will be, the history of the past and of the future, the things I have had and that I will have, all of this awaits us somewhere in this peaceful labyrinth.... I have imagined a magic object, an engraving that would also be a microcosm; *Dante's poem is that picture of universal scope* [emphasis mine]). One of the many things striking about this passage is the extent to which the description of such a universal text is like that of the Aleph, seen by the character Borges in Daneri's cellar and then "written" by the innocent Daneri himself.

3. Petrarch's collection has had a number of names as well as a number of shapes throughout its history; I have relied on and quote Robert Durling's excellent edition and translations, and I prefer the title (also used by Durling) of *Rime sparse*, "Scattered Rhymes," as opposed to *Canzoniere*, rather too simply "Song book," or the more cumbersome Latin *Rerum vulgarium fragmenta*, although all three have been and continue to be used with such regularity—and with differing philological justifications—that it has through usage become more a matter of preference than of any bona fide authenticity.

4. Thiem 1988 is a remarkably useful article, providing not only considerable insights into Borges's relations with Dante but a comprehensive inventory of these relations and a thorough and very helpful bibliography for those of us who are also reversing the expected order of readership: medievalists and Dantisti reading Borges. Stefanini, on the other hand, can be perused as a more typical example of the study that concludes that Borges's treatment is parodic. Among Italianists this is the all too predictable conclusion, since it can scarcely be imagined that serious mockery of Dante—i.e., reservations about his value—could be written by someone like Borges. This is part and parcel of the kind of reverential criticism which has also prevented critics from seeing the ungracious cuts to Arnaut and Pound, and no doubt it is also a part of the post-Frye perception we maintain that when one is writing "criticism" that is the straight stuff, to be taken at face value, like scientific writing. Thus, since Borges's "straight" writing on Dante is almost embarrassingly adoring, he must be "playing" in "The Aleph."

5. Among the most useful I note: Foscolo's 1823 study, interesting and important for obvious historical reasons but also because of his focus on the issue of vernacular as a focal point of both congruence and difference between Dante and Petrarch, and because he is an early critic in the tradition of those who will see the clear antithesis between Beatrice and Laura (a critical tradition which will encompass Freccero 1975 and Vickers 1981); Freccero's now classic and indispensable 1975 "The Fig Tree and the Laurel" and the superb introduction to Durling's edition and translation are in a number of ways critical breakthroughs in dealing with the clearly literary relationship between the Petrarchan corpus and the Dantesque predecessors; Mazzotta 1978 is the study I have found most helpful, with emphasis both on Dante's concept of allegory as Petrarch understood it and on Petrarch's cultivation of a belief in the necessary ambiguity of language; Vickers 1981 emphasizes Petrarch's ability to manipulate two different and potentially contradictory traditions in order to carve out a third and unique place for himself within it; Waller 1980 has a number of insights on the relationship, although she begins with this highly puzzling statement: "Thus we need not deny that Petrarch's poetic originality often takes the shape of a struggle with his precursor Dante, but we need not see his poetry solely in terms of that struggle either" (12). Given how relatively little attention it has been paid, and how diffuse that attention tends to be, this is peculiar. But she often makes telling statements on the relationship, most notably: "Where for Dante error would be more a matter of the reader than of the text, for Petrarch error and its concomitant problems for reading and readability become located in the text itself" (38); see also the incisive and original Shapiro 1980, as well as the more typical, straightforward Sturm-Maddox 1985, who devotes two chapters of her book on Petrarch to the "subtexts" of Dante and provides a detailed and thorough accounting of "Dante in Petrarch"—although she seems scarcely concerned that all of this takes place within a context of specific and insistent denial.

6. The letter itself, *Familiares* XXI, 15, is worth reading in its entirety, as virtually every line of its six or so printed pages is as revealing as an exaggeratedly

staged analytic session could be, beginning with the staggering fact that Dante's name is never even mentioned. The Bernardo 1985 translation is an excellent resource (202–207). There are two detailed studies that do focus on the letter and its implications: the early Bernardo 1955 and Paparelli 1979. The latter, in classic philological fashion, traces out both the history behind the exchange of letters between Boccaccio and Petrarch and the critical reactions to and evaluations of Petrarch's remarkable epistle over the years, from Foscolo's "fascio di contradizzioni, d'ambiguità e d'indirette difese di sé" to Contini's more decorous "ambiguità psicologica." His own assessment is that it is a "masterpiece of hypocrisy" (*capolavoro di ipocrisia*, 77) although his reading of the letter itself more often identifies irony than hypocrisy as such. Paparelli conspicuously does not cite the earlier study by Bernardo (which had appeared in *PMLA*), which, despite the critical naiveté of the moment, is by far the most thorough and, ultimately, most incisive study. It includes considerations of the various possible explanations for Petrarch's stance with respect to Dante, as well as a detailed reading of a different Petrarchan letter, one written to his brother Gherardo, who has entered a monastery, on the difference between the active and the contemplative life (this letter has more recently been analyzed in Mazzotta 1988, who comes to comparable conclusions about it). Bernardo concludes that "for poetry to be great there was really no need to 'dismiss the hypothesis of the active life by reaccepting the contemplative ideal as a superior one' as Dante had done" (499), and that Petrarch believes it is possible to have a vernacular poem which is Christian and yet remain poetry without becoming theology.

7. The incipit that Petrarch uses here is in fact now believed to not have been composed by Arnaut, but it is clear that that was once the attribution and that Petrarch would have thought it Arnaut's. The *sestina* is a *canso* (the Provençal for *canzone*) with an undivided stanza and a number of remarkably challenging rhyme schemes. Detailed discussion of the form, its invention and difficulties can be found in Wilhelm 1982. The one in this *canzone* of Petrarch's is among the least pyrotechnical: a *canso a coblas dissolutas*, where the same rhymes are not used throughout the entire poem. For further details on the different rhyme and metrical schemes used by Petrarch see Durling's introduction.

8. Barolini's recent study (1989) explores this issue extensively and sees the structure itself of the collection, as well as internal thematics, as serving Petrarch's major preoccupation, that of the irrevocable passing of time and coming of death. (The preoccupation with the many different kinds of time and of memory is also crucial in Thomas Greene's rich and powerful reading.) In a discussion of *canzone* 70, Barolini signals that Petrarch's use of other poets' incipits as the final verses of each of the stanzas of this poem is one of Petrarch's many strategies to subvert clear closure. In addition, "most striking is that Petrarch's use of the first verse of his own collection's first *canzone*, 'Nel dolce tempo de la prima etade,' as the last verse of *canzone* 70; thus not only have beginnings become endings, but endings into beginnings, since the *canzone*'s end finds him at the beginning of his own story, at the 'prima etade'" (24).

9. One of the longest-standing exegetical disputes is who the "disdained" one is in *Inferno* 10, the two likeliest being Beatrice or Virgil. Although Freccero makes a convincing case that it is in fact Virgil, I would sustain here that Beatrice echoes no less strongly in Petrarch's reading—a reading, of course, that can readily conflate both.

10. Mazzotta 1978, focused somewhat differently on the "language of the self," provides a number of readings of Petrarch's poetics as reflected in the *Canzoniere*, and particularly as they correspond or not to Dante, that enrich my own reading here. The Petrarch that emerges here, in his struggle with the problem(s) of self, is one whose poetics are those of fragmentation, and for whom and in whom thematic criticism is insufficient (274). Of particular interest and relevance is certainly Mazzotta's reading of another *canzone*, 125, which also directly interweaves the voice of the Dante of the *rime petrose*, a poem, finally, also indicting Dante's poetics, although in this case because they mistake the thrust of the Augustinian theory of language. Once again, the impact of Petrarch's "rebuttal" is that he, Petrarch, is far more astute a literary historian and critic, that he got Augustinian poetics right—he, and not the Dante who claimed, in so many ways, to follow Augustine's teachings and paths.

11. De Man [1964] is an especially helpful reader of Borges in terms of a general "placement": "The least inadequate literary analogy would be with the eighteenth-century *conte philosophique* ... he differs, however, from his eighteenth-century antecedents in that the subject of the stories is the creation of style itself.... His main characters are prototypes for the writer, and his worlds are prototypes for a highly stylized kind of poetry or fiction.... His stories are about the style in which they are written" (23). De Man also emphasizes that Borges is enveloped in the notion that poetic invention and the creative act begin and are rooted in duplicity, and that the appearance of God will signal the end of poetry. How far from Dante!

12. Again Mazzotta provides a similar and supportive reading, even when the focus is somewhat different: "For Petrarch, language is the allegory of desire, a veil, not because it hides a moral meaning but because it always says something else" (291); "To his faith in the mimetic possibilities of language, Petrarch opposes the notion of a radical inadequacy of language. If allegory for Dante (as Petrarch read him) is the envelope of hidden truth and an instrument of knowledge, for Petrarch it is constitutive of language and marks the distance between desire and its signs" (292).

13. The Daneri, as pointed out long ago by Monegal, is a rather conspicuous conflation of Dante Alighieri; see Thiem for a full bibliography and greater detail on the intricacies of Dante allusions. I note also in passing that "first cousin" in Spanish is the far more poetic and less remote *primo hermano*—noteworthy given the intimacy between Daneri and Beatriz that the pathetically jealous Borges vaguely suspects.

14. I think this translation of the crucial "Beatriz se había distraído con

Alvaro" obscures the strong implication in the Spanish that there was an active relationship involved, that Beatriz had amused herself with Alvaro.

15. See the recent psychoanalytical study by Braden (which includes an excellent analysis of Petrarch's dialogue with Augustine in the *Secretum*), who arrives, through a quite different mode of analysis, at conclusions about the *Rime sparse* complementary to those of Mazzotta, quote above: "It is a story in which utterance fails systematically of its ostensible external goal, to double back on its originator" (147). Crucially, Braden outlines the multiple failures of the purported conversion, a conversion for which Petrarch keeps waiting, at least half-heartedly, but that simply will not come; and the fact the greatest poetic effect is that the ultimate external object of desire does not exist except in our imagination (154).

16. In his most recent meditation on poetry, *Ruin the Sacred Truths*, the always provocative Bloom offers a reading of Dante that in texture resonates more strongly of Borges as a kind of answer to his reading than of the conventional academic readings of recent years: Dante, a preternaturally strong poet, is both prophetic and very much the creator of his own universe, and his Beatrice is "at the center of an idiosyncratic gnosis" (47). In this universe, a universe in which the commonplace distinctions between sacred and secular in textuality are spurious, Dante is also an Aleph, but, crucially, an Aleph that is nakedly magical: one poet's construct and thus personal revelation. Oddly enough, Bloom too sees fit to close his own meditations on the *Divine Comedy* with the image of Beatrice's smile (a Beatrice who is the final and singular guide because she is so explicitly his own creation): "Freud ... lamented his failure to cure those who would not accept the cure ... Dante too would not owe any man anything, not even if the man were Virgil, his poetic father.... The cure was accepted by Dante from his physician, Beatrice, but she was his own creation, the personal myth that centered his poem. In smiling and looking at him as they part, she confirms the cure" (50).

17. Petrarch's letter to Boccaccio, after several preliminary sentences, gets to the matter at hand as follows: "In the first place, you ask pardon, somewhat heatedly, for seeming to praise unduly a fellow countryman of ours who is popular for his poetic style but doubtless noble for his theme; and you beg pardon for this as though I believe that praises for him or for anyone else would detract from my personal glory" (Bernardo, ed. and trans. 1985:202). For a discussion of the vexing problem of Dante's very long shadow in the context of the history of later Italian literature see chapter 2 above.

18. "... these silly admirers who never know why they praise or censure, who so mispronounce and mangle his verses that they could do no greater injury to a poet ..." (Bernardo 1985:204–5).

19. Tanturli believes that Petrarch was the first in several hundred years of Italians—Renaissance Humanists—to disdain Dante because of their disdain for the *volgare* itself.

20. Petrarch's multiple and variegated affinities with Latin America are

beginning to surface as a subject of critical interest: Professor Roland Greene of Harvard, for example, is currently engaged in a project exploring the relations between Petrarchan discourse and the colonial enterprise, particularly how the ethics of Petrarchism operate as a crucial language in the earliest colonial texts. I am grateful to the author for sharing his work-in-progress thoughts with me.

21. See Petrie's lucid discussion of Petrarch's belief in the importance of imitation, particularly of the Augustan poets, as well as her comments on the related problem of the acquisition of fame.

22. This necessary clarification—and limitation—of what can possibly be called Dante's "influence" appears in the first essay of a collection devoted to "Dante Among the Moderns" (McDougal, ed. 1986) and is especially welcome given the tendency, very much apparent in the introduction to that volume, to see Dante as a highly "influential" poet in the conventional sense of the word.

23. Nancy Vickers has been doing extraordinary work in the last several years on the dispersal—the inevitable process of illegitimization—of Petrarch in contemporary music, a dispersal due in great measure to the fact that Petrarchism spread far beyond the "high" cultural content within which it is normally studied (Vickers 1988).

Chronology

1899	Jorge Luis Borges is born on August 24 in Buenos Aires to Jorge Guillermo Borges and Leonor Acevedo de Borges.
1899–1914	Borges is primarily educated at home by his parents, English grandmother, and English tutor.
1914	The Borges family travels to Europe. At the outbreak of World War I, they stay in Geneva, Switzerland, where Borges attends secondary school.
1919	Borges travels with his family in Spain, and he publishes several poems under the influence of the Spanish *Ultraísta* movement.
1921	The Borges family returns to Argentina. Borges founds, edits, and publishes work in literary magazines.
1923	Publishes *Fervor de Buenos Aires*, his first book of poems. Makes a second trip to Europe.
1924	Returns to Buenos Aires.
1925	Publishes *Luna de Enfrente* (*Moon Across the Way*), his second book of poems. First essay collection, *Inquisiciones*, appears.
1926	*El tamaño di mi esperanza* (*The Size of My Hope*), essays, is published.
1928	*El idioma de los argentinos* (*The Language of the Argentines*), essays, is published.
1929	Publishes *Cauderno San Martín*, poems; wins second prize in the Buenos Aires municipal literary contest.

1930	Publishes *Evaristo Carriego*. A right-wing army coup deposes the Radical government of Hipólito Irigoyen.
1932	Publishes *Discusión*, essays.
1933	Appointed literary editor for weekly arts supplement of *Crítica*, a tabloid.
1935	Borges's grandmother, Frances Haslam de Borges, dies. Publishes *Historia universal de la infamia* (*A Universal History of Infamy*).
1936	Publishes *Historia de la eternidad* (*A History of Eternity*), a collection of essays.
1937	Obtains a job as First Assistant in the Miguel Cané branch of the Municipal Library, a position he would hold for nine years.
1938	Borges's father dies. On Christmas Eve, Borges injures his head and falls ill with septicemia; during recovery, he writes stories.
1939	Writes "Pierre Menard, Author of *Don Quixote*," generally considered the first real "Borgesian" story.
1941	Publishes *El jardín de senderos que se bifurcan* (*The Garden of Forking Paths*).
1942	Publishes *Six Problems for Don Isidro Parodi*, co-written with Adolfo Bioy-Casares under the joint pen-name of "Bustos Domecq." The magazine *Sur* dedicates special issue to Borges.
1944	Publishes *Ficciones*. Receives "Prize of Honor" from the Sociedad Argentina de Escritores.
1946	Resigns from his Library position when General Juan Domingo Perón gains power. Accepts a number of teaching and lecturing jobs.
1949	Publishes *The Aleph*.
1950	Borges is Elected President of the Sociedad Argentina de Escritores.
1951	*Ficciones* is published in Paris—first foreign translation of a Borges publication.
1952	Publishes *Otras inquisiciones* (*Other Inquisitions*), essays; Eva Perón dies.

1955	Appointed Director of the National Library after Perón falls; Borges becomes almost completely blind.
1956	Named to the professorship of English and American Literature at the University of Buenos Aires, a position he would hold for twelve years. Receives honorary doctorate from the University of Cuyo. Awarded the National Prize for Literature.
1957	Publishes *Manual de zoología fantastica* (*A Handbook of Fantastic Zoology*) with Margarita Guerrero.
1960	Publishes *El hacedor* (English version *Dreamtigers*).
1961	Shares the Formentor Prize with Samuel Beckett, bringing him international recognition; is invited to the University of Texas as Visiting Professor.
1962	*Labyrinths* and *Ficciones*, the first English collections of Borges's work, are published.
1963	Travels and lectures in England, France, Spain, and Switzerland.
1964	Publishes *El Otro, el mismo*, poems.
1967	Marries Elsa Astete Millán; is invited to teach at Harvard University as Charles Eliot Norton Lecturer.
1968	*El libro de los seres imaginarios* (*The Book of Imaginary Beings*) is published.
1969	Publishes *Elogio de la sombra* (In Praise of Darkness), poetry.
1970	Publishes *El informe de Brodie* (*Dr. Brodie's Report*), stories; separates from Elsa.
1971	Receives an honorary degree from Columbia University and Oxford University. Wins the Jerusalem Prize. Travels throughout the United States and Europe.
1972	Publishes *El oro de los tigres* (The Gold of the Tigers), prose and poems.
1973	Resigns as Director of the National Library after Perón regains the presidency.
1974	*Obras completas* is published.
1975	Publishes *El libro de arena* (*The Book of Sand*), stories; *La rosa profunda* (*The Deep Rose*), poems. Borges's mother

	dies at age 99. Perón dies, and is succeeded by his widow, Isabel.
1976	Publishes *La moneda de hierro (The Iron Coin)*, poetry; *Crónicas de Buestos Domecq* (*Chronicles of Bustos Domecq*), co-authored with Adolfo Bioy Casares. Right-wing army coup overthrows government of Isabel Perón.
1977	Publishes *Historia de la noche*, poems.
1979	Travels to Japan. Receives the Gold medal from the Académie Françiase and the Order of Merit from the Federal Republic of Germany; Receives Cross of the Falcon from the government of Iceland.
1980	Travels to Spain, is awarded the Cervantes Prize.
1981	Awarded the Ablazan Prize in Rome; Awarded the Ollín Yoliztli Prize in Mexico City; Receives Honorary Doctorate from Harvard University.
1983	Awarded the Légion d'Honneur.
1984	Travels in Italy, Japan, Greece; *Atlas* is published.
1985	Moves to Geneva, Switzerland. Publishes *Los conjurados*, (*The Conspirators*), poetry and prose.
1986	Marries personal assistant, María Kodama. Dies in Geneva on June 14.

Works by Jorge Luis Borges

Fervor de Buenos Aires, 1923.
Inquisiciones, 1925.
Luna de enfrente, 1925.
El tamaño de mi esperanza, 1926.
El idioma de los argentinos, 1928.
Cuaderno San Martín, 1929.
Evaristo Carriego, 1930.
Discusión, 1932.
Historia universal de la infamia, 1935.
Historia de la eternidad, 1936.
El jardín de los senderos que se bifurcan, 1941.
Poemas, 1943, 1943.
Ficciones (1935–1944), 1944.
Nueva refutación del tiempo, 1947.
El Aleph, 1949.
Otras inquisiciones (1937–1952), 1952.
El hacedor, 1960.
Antología personal, 1961.
Obra poética (1923–1964), 1964.
Para las seis cuerdas, 1965.

El libro de los seres imaginarios. Margarita Guerrero, co-author, 1967.

Nueva antología personal, 1968.

Elogio de la sombra, 1969.

El otro, el mismo, 1969.

El informe de Brodie, 1970.

El libro de arena, 1975.

La rosa profunda, 1975.

La moneda de hierro, 1976.

Historia de la noche, 1977.

Obras completas en colaboración, 1979.

Obra poética: 1923–1976, 1979.

La cifra, 1981.

Nueva ensayos dantescos, 1982.

Vienticinco agosto 1983 y otros ceuntos, 1983.

Los conjurados, 1985.

Principal Translations in English

Ficciones. trans. Anthony Kerrigan and others, 1962.

Labyrinths: Selected Stories and Other Writings. Eds. Donald A. Yates and James E. Irby. 1962.

Dreamtigers (El hacedor). Trans. Mildred Boyer and Harold Morland. 1964.

Other Inquisitions 1937–1952. Trans. Ruth L.C. Simms. 1964.

A Personal Anthology. Ed. Anthony Kerrigan. 1967.

The Aleph and Other Stories: 1933–1969. Ed. and Trans. Norman Thomas di Giovanni in collaboration with the author. 1970.

The Book of Imaginary Beings. Margarita Guerrero, coauthor. Trans. Norman Thomas di Giovanni in collaboration with the author. 1970.

Doctor Brodie's Report. Trans. Norman Thomas di Giovanni in collaboration with the author. 1972.

Selected Poems 1923–1967. Trans. Norman Thomas di Giovanni. 1972.

A Universal History of Infamy. Trans. Norman Thomas di Giovanni. 1972.

In Praise of Darkness. Trans. Norman Thomas di Giovanni. 1974.

The Book of Sand. Trans. Norman Thomas di Giovanni. 1977.

The Gold of the Tigers: Selected Later Poems. Trans. Alastair Reid. 1977.

Evaristo Carriego: A Book about Old-Time Buenos Aires. Trans. Norman Thomas di Giovanni. 1983.

Atlas. Trans. Anthony Kerrigan. 1985.

Ficciones. Intro. John Sturrock. 1993

Collected Fictions. Trans. Andrew Hurley. 1998.

Selected Non-Fiction. Eliot Weinberger, ed. 1999.

Works about
Jorge Luis Borges

Agheana, Ian T. *The Meaning of Experience in the Prose of Jorge Luis Borges.* New York: Peter Lang, 1988.

Aizenberg, Edna, ed. *Borges and His Successors: The Borgesian Impact on Literature and the Arts.* Columbia: University of Missouri Press, 1990.

———. *The Aleph Weaver: Biblical, Kabbalistic and Judaic Elements in Borges.* Potomac, MD: Scripta Humanistica, 1984.

Alazraki, Jaime, ed. *Critical Essays on Jorge Luis Borges.* Boston: G.K. Hall, 1987.

———. *Borges and the Kabbalah: And Other Essays on His Fiction and Poetry.* Cambridge: Cambridge University Press, 1988.

Balderston, Daniel. *The Literary Universe of Jorge Luis Borges: An Index to References and Allusions to Persons, Titles, and Places in his Writings.* Westport, CT: Greenwood, 1986.

———. *Out of Context: Historical Reference and the Representation of Reality in Borges.* Durham: Duke University Press, 1993.

Barnstone, Willis. *Borges at Eighty: Conversations.* Bloomington: Indiana University Press, 1982.

Barrenechea, Ana María. *Borges the Labyrinth Maker.* Trans. Robert Lima. New York: New York University Press, 1965.

Barth, John. "The Literature of Exhaustion." *Atlantic Monthly* (August 1967): 29–34.

Bell-Villada, Gene H. *Borges and His Fiction: A Guide to His Mind and Art.* Revised Edition. Austin: University of Texas Press, 1999.

Block de Behar, Lisa. *The Passion of an Endless Quotation.* Trans. William Egginton. New York: State University of New York Press, 2003.

Bloom, Harold, ed. *Modern Critical Views: Jorge Luis Borges*. Philadelphia: Chelsea House, 1986.

———, ed. *Major Short Story Writers: Jorge Luis Borges*. Philadelphia: Chelsea House, 2002.

Burgin, Richard. *Conversations with Jorge Luis Borges*. New York: Holt, Rinehart and Winston, 1969.

Christ, Ronald. *The Narrow Act: Borges' Art of Allusion*. New York: New York University Press, 1969. (2nd ed., New York: Lumen Books, 1995).

———. "The Art of Fiction: Jorge Luis Borges." *Paris Review 40* (1967): 116–64.

Crossan, John Dominic. *Raid on the Articulate: Comic Eschatology in Jesus and Borges*. New York: Harper & Row, 1976.

de Man, Paul. "A Modern Master." *New York Review of Books* 3, no. 6 (1964).

di Giovanni, Norman Thomas, and others. *Borges on Writing*. New York: Dutton, 1973.

———, ed. *In Memory of Borges*. London: Constable, 1988.

Donoso, José. *The Boom in Spanish American Literature: A Personal History*. trans. G. Kolovakos. New York: Columbia University Press, 1977.

Dunham, Lowell, and Ivar Ivask, eds. *The Cardinal Points of Borges*. Norman: University of Oklahoma Press, 1971.

Echevarría, Roberto González. *Myth and Archive: A Theory of Latin American Narrative*. Cambridge: Cambridge University Press, 1990.

———, ed. *The Oxford Book of Latin American Short Stories*. New York: Oxford University Press, 1997.

Echevarria, Roberto Gonzalez and Enrique Pupo-Walker. *The Cambridge History of Latin American Literature*. 3 vols. Cambridge: Cambridge University Press, 1995.

Fishburn, Evelyn and Psiche Hughes. *A Dictionary of Borges*. (Foreword by Mario Vargas Llosa and Anthony Burgess). London: Duckworth, 1990.

Foster, David William. *Studies in the Contemporary Spanish American Short Story*. Columbia: University of Missouri Press, 1979.

Fuentes, Carlos. "The Accidents of Time" in *The Borges Tradition*. ed. Norman Thomas di Giovanni. London: Constable, 1995: 49–69.

Gass, W.H. "Imaginary Borges." *New York Review of Books*, 20 November 1969: 5–8.

Hernández Martín, Jorge. *Readers and Labyrinths*. New York: Garland, 1995.

Jaén, Didier T. "The Esoteric Tradition in Borges' 'Tlön, Uqbar, Orbis Tertius'." *Studies in Short Fiction* 21 (Winter 1984): 25–39.

———. *Borges' Esoteric Library: Metaphysics to Metafiction*. Lanham, Maryland: University Press of America, 1992.

Kodama de Borges, María. "Jorge Luis Borges, Religions and the Mystical Experience." In *Jorge Luis Borges: Thought and Knowledge in the XXth Century*. eds. Alfonso de Toro and Fernando de Toro. Frankfurt: Vervuert, 1999: 15–27.

Lindstrom, Naomi. *Jorge Luis Borges: A Study of the Short Fiction*. Boston: Twayne Publishers, 1990.

Menocal, María Rosa. *Writing in Dante's Cult of Truth: From Borges to Boccaccio*. Durham: Duke University Press, 1991.

McMurray, George R. *Jorge Luis Borges*. New York: Frederick Ungar Publishing Co., 1980.

Merrell, Floyd. *Unthinking Thinking: Jorge Luis Borges, Mathematics and the New Physics*. West Lafayette, IN: Purdue University Press, 1991.

Molloy, Silvia. *Signs of Borges*. Durham: Duke University Press, 1994.

Rodman, Selden. *Tongues of Fallen Angels: Conversations with Jorge Luis Borges*. New York: New Directions Publishing, 1974.

Rodriguez Monegal, Emir. *Jorge Luis Borges: A Literary Biography*. New York: Dutton, 1978.

Rodríguez-Luis, Julio. *The Contemporary Praxis of the Fantastic: Borges and Cortazar*. New York: Garland Publishing, 1991.

Sarlo, Beatriz. *Jorge Luis Borges: the Writer on the Edge*. New York: Verso, 1993.

Sorrentino, Fernando. *Seven Conversations with Jorge Luis Borges*. trans. Clark M. Zlotchew. Troy, NY: Whitson, 1982.

Stabb, Martin S. *Borges Revisited*. Boston: Twayne Publishers, 1991.

Stewart, Jon. "Borges on Immortality." *Philosophy and Literature*. 17 (October 1993): 295–301.

Sturrock, John. *Paper Tigers: The Ideal Fictions of Jorge Luis Borges*. Oxford: Clarendon, 1977.

Thiem, Jon. "Borges, Dante, and the Poetics of Total Vision."

Comparative Literature 40 (Spring 1988): 97–121.

Triquarterly 25 (1972). Special Issue on Borges. Reprinted as *Prose for Borges*.

Updike, John. "Books: The Author as Librarian." *New Yorker* (30 October 1965): 223–46.

Urraca, Beatriz. "Wor(l)ds Through the Looking-Glass: Borges's Mirrors and Contemporary Theory." *Revista Canadiense de Estudios Hispánicos*. 17 (Otoño 1992): 153–76.

Wheelock, Carter. *The Mythmaker: A Study of Motif and Symbol in the Short Stories of Jorge Luis Borges*. Austin: University of Texas Press, 1969.

Woodall, James. *Borges: A Life*. New York: Basic Books, 1996.

Websites

Jorge Luis Borges Center for Studies and Documentation
http://www.hum.aau.dk/Institut/rom/borges/borges.htm

Jorge Luis Borges: The Garden of Forking Paths
http://www.themodernword.com/borges/

The Jorge Luis Borges Collection—University of Virginia Library
http://www.lib.virginia.edu/speccol/collections/borges.html

Contributors

HAROLD BLOOM is Sterling Professor of the Humanities at Yale University. He is the author of over 20 books, including *Shelley's Mythmaking* (1959), *The Visionary Company* (1961), *Blake's Apocalypse* (1963), *Yeats* (1970), *A Map of Misreading* (1975), *Kabbalah and Criticism* (1975), *Agon: Toward a Theory of Revisionism* (1982), *The American Religion* (1992), *The Western Canon* (1994), and *Omens of Millennium: The Gnosis of Angels, Dreams, and Resurrection* (1996). *The Anxiety of Influence* (1973) sets forth Professor Bloom's provocative theory of the literary relationships between the great writers and their predecessors. His most recent books include *Shakespeare: The Invention of the Human* (1998), a 1998 National Book Award finalist, *How to Read and Why* (2000), *Genius: A Mosaic of One Hundred Exemplary Creative Minds* (2002), and *Hamlet: Poem Unlimited* (2003). In 1999, Professor Bloom received the prestigious American Academy of Arts and Letters Gold Medal for Criticism, and in 2002 he received the Catalonia International Prize.

AMY SICKELS is a writer living in New York City. She received her Master of Fine Arts in Creative Writing from Penn State University.

ELIZABETH BEAUDIN received her Ph.D. from Yale in 1995. She is a medievalist specializing in the treatment of love and love-sickness in early Spanish and Hispano-Arabic texts.

PAUL DE MAN was Sterling Professor of French at Yale University. Among his many contributions to literary scholarship are *Blindness and Insight*, *Allegories of Reading*, and *The Rhetoric of Romanticism*.

JAIME ALAZRAKI, Professor of Spanish at Columbia University, has written numerous scholarly works on major Latin American writers throughout his distinguished career including *La prosa narrativa de Jorge Luis Borges*, and *Narrativa y crítica de nuestra América*, and has edited several collections of critical essays on Borges and Julio Cortázar.

MARÍA ROSA MENOCAL is the R. Selden Rose Professor of Spanish and the Director of the Whitney Humanities Center at Yale University. Menocal is the author of *The Arabic Role in Medieval Literary History: A Forgotten Heritage*, *Shards of Love: Exile and the Origins of the Lyric*, and co-editor of the *Cambridge History of Arabic Literature: Al-Andalus*. Her latest work is *The Ornament of the World: How Muslims, Jews, and Christians Created a Culture of Tolerance in Medieval Spain*.

INDEX

"Acercamiento a Almotásim, El (The Approach to al-Mu'tasim)," 21
   hoax story, 62, 83
Adventures of Huckleberry Finn (Twain), 9
Alazraki, Jaime, 145
   on Borges and modernism, 79–90
Aleph, El, 31, 40, 82–84, 93–94, 134, 137
   Dante in, 97, 108–9, 111–22, 124
   irony in, 3
   themes in, 30, 56–57, 59–61, 76
Aleph and Other Stories: 1933–1969, The, 118, 138
Antologia personal (A Personal Anthology), 58, 60, 63–67, 137–38
"Approach to al-Mu'tasim, The." *See* "Acercamiento a Almotásim, El"
Aristotle, 83
"Art of Poetry, The." *See* "Arte Poética"
"Arte Poética (The Art of Poetry)"
   time theme, 57–58
Atlas, 49, 136, 139
Augustine, 52
Aurelius, Marcus, 52
"Autobiographical Essay," 41, 43

Back to Methuselah (Shaw), 3
Barth, John, 35, 81, 88
Barthelme, Donald, 35

Barthes, Roland, 85–86
Beaudin, Elizabeth, 145
   on Borge's time theme, 51–70
Beckett, Samuel, 34, 79, 87
Bioy-Casares, Adolfo, 134, 136
Bishop, John Peale, 71
Blake, William, 29, 83
Bloom, Harold, 145
   introduction, 1–4
   work in the writer, ix–xiii
Book of Imaginary Beings, The. *See Libro de los seres imaginarios, El*
Book of Sand, The. *See Libro de arena, El*
Borges, Jorge Luis
   awards, 28, 33–34, 135–36, 39, 42, 47–48
   biography of, 5–50
   birth, 5, 7–8, 133
   blindness, 6–7, 22, 29, 31–33, 35, 42–43, 49, 63–64, 83, 88
   chronology, 133–36
   criticism, 1–6, 25–26, 30, 33, 42–43, 45–48, 50–53, 61, 71, 78, 97, 119
   death, 45, 50, 136
   education, 9–12, 44, 133
   family, 6–16, 18–19, 21–26, 28–30, 32, 35–39, 41–42, 46, 50, 133–35
   imagination, 6–7, 9–10, 26, 52, 57, 66–676

147

influenced by, 6–22, 35–36, 38–42, 44–45, 47, 51–53, 83
lecturing, 29–30, 33, 35, 37, 39, 41, 45
marriages, 38–39, 135–36, 40–42, 45, 49–50
and modernism, 79–90
and politics, 26–31, 33, 35, 42–50, 64
poetic influence, 2, 35, 50, 83, 86–87, 91, 95–96
relationship to Dante, 91–97, 99, 102, 104, 108–26
relationship to Petrarch, 94–97, 99, 102, 104, 108–11, 115, 118–26
style, 73, 77, 80–82, 85, 88
works about, 141–44
works by, 133, 137–39
"Borges and I"
 dual identities theme, 62, 64, 74
 Borges persona in, 34, 44, 62, 64
Brothers Grimm, 10
Browne, Thomas, 78
Browning, Robert, 2, 80
Buckley, William, 79
Burton, Richard, 55, 61

Caillois, Roger, 28
Camus, Albert, 73, 86
Cansinos-Assens, Rafael
 influence on Borges, 13–17, 36
Canto, Estela, 27–29
Canto general (Neruda), 3
Caraffa, Alfredo Brandán, 17
Carlyle, Thomas, 12, 54
Carroll, Lewis, 10, 55, 57, 83
Casares, Aldofo Bioy, 25
 influence on Borges, 20–22, 30, 38–40, 47
Cervantes, Miguel de, 10, 29, 51, 53–54, 74–76
Chesterton, G.K., 83–84

Cifra, La, 138
"Circular Ruins, The." *See* "Ruinas Circulares, La"
"Circular Time"
 time theme in, 52, 58
Collected Fictions, 60, 62, 64–65, 139
Commedia (Dante), 93, 97, 100–2, 116, 122, 125
"Conjectural Poem"
 power of Juan Domingo Perón, 26
Conjurados, Los (*The Conspirators*), 136, 138
Conrad, Joseph, 54
Conspirators, The. See Conjurados, Los
Coover, Robert, 35
Cortázar, Julio, 5, 35, 79
"Craft of Verse, The"
 lectures, 39
Crane, Hart, 71
Cuaderno San Martin, 18, 133, 137
Cummings, E.E., 71

Dante, 23, 51–52, 65
 relationship to Borges, 91–97, 99, 102, 104, 108–11, 113–16, 118–26
 relationship to Petrarch, 94–111, 115, 118–26
"Dead Man, The," 84
"Death and the Compass"
 cabbalism, 1
 infamy theme, 76, 83
Deep Rose, The. See Rosa profunda, La
Dickens, Charles, 10, 51
Dickinson, Emily, 27
Discusión, 20, 82, 134, 137
Divine Comedy (Dante), 23, 124
Doctor Brodie's Report. See Informe de Brodie, El
Don Quixote (Cervantes), 54, 61, 76
Dreamtigers. See Hacedor, El
Dual identities theme, 63, 74–78

"Duración del infierno, La (Duration of Hell, The)"
time theme in, 52
"Duration of Hell, The." *See* "Duración del infierno, La"
"Elementos de preceptiva," 81, 85, 87
Elogio de la sombra (*In Praise of Darkness*), 40–41, 135, 138–39
Emerson, Ralph Waldo, 1, 79
"End, The," 83
"Esfera de Pascal, La (Pascal's Sphere)"
metaphors and space in, 52
time theme, 59
"Espejo de los enigmas, El (Mirror of Enigmas, The)"
time theme in, 52
Evaristo Carriego: A Book about Old-Time Buenos Aires, 19, 134, 137, 139
childhood in, 9

Fascism, 2, 22, 25, 27
Fajardo, Saavedra, 80
Faulkner, William, 23, 28, 71
"Feeling in Death." *See* "Sentirse en muerte"
Fernández, Macedonio
influence on Borges, 15–17
Fervor de Buenos Aires, 16, 133, 137
Ficciones, 6, 25, 28, 30, 35, 38, 40, 55, 60, 62, 77, 82–83, 134–35, 137–39
Flaubert, Gustave, 12
"Flower of Coleridge, The," 81
"For Bernard Shaw," 85
Freud, Sigmund, 1–2
Fuentes, Carlos, 35
"Funes the Memorious," 76
Futurism, 14

Garden of Forking Paths, The. *See Jardín de los senderos que se bifurcan, El*
Genette, Gérard, 87
Gide, André, 19, 72
Giovanni, Norma Thomas di
influence on Borges, 39–42, 45
Gold of the Tigers: Selected Later Poems, The. *See Oro de los tiges, El*
Góngora, 80
Gnostic vision
in Borges, 1–2, 4, 25, 54
in Kafka, 1
Guerrero, Concepción, 16–17
Guerrero, Margarita, 135
Guibert, Rita
on Borges, 43
Güiraldes, Ricardo, 17

Hacedor, El (*Dreamtigers*), 38, 40, 62, 71, 74, 77–78, 135, 137
composition, 34
Handbook of Fantastic Zoology, A. *See Manual de zoologia fantastica*
Hawthorne, Nathaniel, 4
Hernández, José, 10, 83
Historia de la eternidad (*A History of Eternity*), 21, 62, 80, 137
time theme in, 52
Historia de la noche, 136, 138
Historia universal de la infamia (*A Universal History of Infamy*), 21, 137, 72, 77, 81–82, 87, 139
History of Eternity, A. *See Historia de la eternidad*
Homer, 3, 51, 80, 121
Hume, 52, 65
Huxley, Aldous, 19
Hydrothapia, Urne-Buriall (Browne), 78

Ibarra, Néstor
  influence on Borges, 19–20, 27–28
Idealism, 2–3, 14
Idioma de los argentinos, El (*The Language of the Argentines*), 18–19, 82, 137
"Immortal, The"
  infamy theme, 76, 83
  irony, 3
Infamy theme, 71–78, 82
Informe de Brodie, El (*Doctor Bodie's Report*), 135, 138
  Argentina concern, 40
  narratives, 40, 84
In Praise of Darkness. See *Elogio de la sombra*
Inquisiciones, 17, 19, 82, 133, 137
Invention of Morel, The (Casares), 26
Iron Coin, The. See *Moneda de hierro, La*

James, Henry, 28, 54
Jardín de los senderos que se bifurcan, El (*The Garden of Forking Paths*), 137
  criticism, 26
  infamy theme, 73, 76
  labyrinth of ideas, 25, 73
  narrative techniques, 25
Joyce, James, 80, 88
Jung, Carl, 1, 79–80

Kafka, Franz, 1–2, 28, 71, 73, 80, 87, 95
Kazin, Alfred, 79
Keats, John, 10
Kipling, Rudyard, 10, 44
Klee, Paul, 18
Kodama, Maria, 45, 47, 49136

Labyrinths: Selected Stories and Other Writings, 30, 59–60, 62, 64–67, 71, 73–76, 78, 135, 138

Labyrinth theme, 1–2, 4, 25, 73
Language of the Argentines The. See *Idioma de los argentinos, El*
Latin American literature, 5, 14, 16, 35, 42, 50, 71
Leaves of Grass (Whitman)
  influence on Borges, 12, 48
"Library of Babel, The"
  allegory, 25
  narrative, 83
Libro de arena, El (*The Book of Sand*), 47, 135, 138–39
Libro de los seres imaginarios, El (*The Book of Imaginary Beings*), 40, 135, 138
"Life of Tadeo Isidoro Cruz, The," 83
"Limits"
  subject, 3
London, Jack, 10
Longfellow, Henry Wadsworth, 10
Lorca, García Federico, 21
Luna de enfrente (*Moon Across the Way*), 17, 133, 137

Magias parciales del Quijote, 53
Mallarmé, 12
Man, Paul de, 126, 145
  on Borge's infamy theme, 71–78
  on Borges dual identities theme, 74–78
Manual de zoologia fantastica (*A Handbook of Fantastic Zoology*), 135
Mariani, Roberto, 17
Márquez, Gabriel García, 5, 35, 91
Marxism, 2, 48
Masters, Edgar Lee, 71
Mastronardi, Carlos, 18
Maupassant, Guy de, 12
Maurosis, André, 79
Melville, Herman, 28, 79
"Memoria de Shakespeare, La (Shakespeare's Memory)"

Menocal, María Rosa, 145
  on the relationship of Borges, Dante, Petrarch, 91–132
Millán, Elsa Astete, 18, 38–39, 41, 45, 50, 135
Milton, John, 35
"Mirror of Enigmas, The." *See* "Espejo de los enigmas, El"
Modernism, 14, 20
  and Borges, 79–90
Moneda de hierro, La (*The Iron Coin*), 136, 138
Monegal, Emir Rodríguez
  on Borges, 29, 32, 46
Moon Across the Way. See Luna de Enfrente
Mysticism and metaphysics, 6, 20–21, 25, 30, 35, 52–53, 57, 63–65, 67, 82

Nationalism, 26
Neruda, Pablo, 3, 21, 48
"New Refutation of Time, The." *See* "Nueva refutación del tiempo"
Nietzsche, 103
Nueva antologia personal, 67, 138
Nueva ensayos dantescos, 104, 138
"Nueva refutación del tiempo (The New Refutation of Time)", 137
  narrative, 64–65

Obra poética, 38, 137–38
Obras completas en colaboración, 47, 138
Ocampo, Victoria
  influence on Borges, 19
Oro de los tiges, El (*Gold of the Tigers: Selected Later Poems, The*), 139
"Other Dead, The," 84
Other Inquisitions. See Otras inquisiciones
Otras inquisiciones (*Other Inquisitions*), 30, 52–53, 64, 134, 137–38
Otro, el mismo, El, 67, 135, 138
Out of the Silent Planet (Lewis), 24

"Page to Commemorate Colonel Suárez, Victor at Junín"
  dual identities theme, 63
Para las seis cuerdas, 137
"Partial Magic of the *Quixote*"
  time theme, 53, 55, 57, 65
"Pascal's Sphere." *See* "Esfera de Pascal, La"
Paz, Pablo Rojas, 17
Perón, Juan Domingo, 26–31, 45–47
Personal Anthology, A. See Antologia personal
Petrarch
  relationship to Borges, 96–97, 99, 102, 104, 108–11, 115, 117–26
  relationship to Dante, 96–111, 115, 118–26
Phantasmagoria, 1
"Pierre Menard, Author of *Don Quixote*," 33–34
  Borges on, 2, 62
  dual identities theme, 74–77
  hoax story, 25, 62, 81
  infamy theme, 74–77
  narrative, 62, 87
  time theme in, 54, 61
Platonism, 2, 52
Poe, Edgar Allan, 10, 44, 79, 83
"Poem of the Gifts." *See* "Poema de los dones, El"
"Poema de los dones, El (Poem of the Gifts)"
  dual identities theme, 63
  irony in, 31
Poemas, 137
  allegory, 26
"Poetry of Guido Cavalcanti," 95
Postmodernism, 35

and Borges, 5
Pynchon, Thomas, 35

Realism, 5, 20, 25, 77
Rebel, The, 86
"Recoleta Cemetery"
　doubled identities in, 63
Reyes, Alfonso
　influence on Borges, 17, 19
Rimbaud, Arthur, 12
Rime sparse (Petrarch), 97–99, 107, 110, 117–19, 122, 124, 126
Rosa profunda, La (*The Deep Rose*), 135, 138
"Ruinas Circulares, La (The Circular Ruins)," 83
　time theme, 55, 59
Russell, Bertrand, 52

Sartor Resartus (Carlyle)
　influence on Borges, 12
Sartre, 73
Schopenhauer, 52, 65
Selected Non-Fiction, 66–67, 139
Selected Poems (1923–1967), 58, 63, 68, 139
"Sentirse en muerte (Feeling in Death)"
　time theme, 65–66
Shakespeare, William, 3, 37, 51, 75, 86
"Shakespeare's Memory." *See* "Memoria de Shakespeare, La"
"Shape of the Sword, The"
　infamy theme, 73, 75
Shaw, George Bernard, 3, 27–28, 83
Shelley, Percy, 10, 81
Sickles, Amy, 145
　biography on Borges, 5–50
Six Problems for Don Isidro Parodi, 26, 134

Size of My Hope, The. *See Tamañde mi esperanza, El*
Solari, Alejandro Schulz, 18
"South, The." *See* Sur, El
"Spinoza"
　metaphysics, 67–68
Sterberg, Josef von, 83
Stevens, Wallace, 71
Stevenson, Robert Louis, 10, 83
"Streetcorner Man," 20–21, 83
"Sur, El (The South)"
　dream and reality in, 3, 61
Swineburne, Algernon Charles, 10
Symbolism, 12, 73

Tamañde mi esperanza, El (*The Size of My Hope*), 17, 19, 137
"Theme of the Traitor and the Hero," 75
Thousand Nights and a Night, A (anonymous)
　influence on Borges, 9, 51–55, 57, 61, 67, 72, 76
"Three Versions of Judas," 83
Through the Looking-Glass (Carroll), 55
Time theme, 51–70
"Tlön, Uqbar, Orbis Tertius," 60
　dual identities theme, 75
　infamy theme, 73, 75–76
　irony in, 2
　metaphor for global catastrophe, 25
Tolstoy, Leo, 84
Twain, Mark, 51
　influence on Borges, 9, 44

"Ulrike"
　love story, 47
Ultraism, 14, 16–18, 20
Universal History of Infamy, A. *See Historia universal de la infamia*

Valéry, 81
Vazquez, Mariá Esther, 37–38
Vienticinco agosto 1983 y otros ceuntos, 138
Virgil, 110, 121
Vita nuova (Dante), 100, 102, 116

Wells, H.G., 10, 83
Whitman, Walt
   influence on Borges, 12–13, 48, 117–18

Wilde, Oscar, 10, 44
Woodall, James
   on Borges, 10–11, 14, 16, 19–21, 26–29, 35–37, 40–41, 43, 46–47, 49
Woolf, Virginia, 23, 36

"Zahir, The," 59
   dream and reality in, 60
   infamy theme, 76
Zola, Emíle, 12